SMART DIY: BOOK III

The Finish-Line ADU:

Let the Pros Build the Box, You Make It a Home

Smart DIY - Volume III

Written by Thomas Quirk
Edited by Angélica Díaz
Review and Design by Angélica Díaz

First Edition: 2026
Production:

SMART DIY: BOOK III

The Finish-Line ADU:

Let the Pros Build the Box, You Make It a Home

CONTENT

INTRODUCTION

WHY YOUR ADU ESTIMATE IS WRONG

After reviewing hundreds of ADU proposals, bids, and completed projects across Southern California, one pattern appears again and again: the first number homeowners are given is almost never the real number. Most people decide to build an Accessory Dwelling Unit for practical reasons—to generate rental income, house a family member, or increase property value—and at the beginning the costs often sound manageable, with many being told their ADU will cost between $150,000 and $200,000. Then reality hits, and by the time construction is complete, that original estimate has grown to $350,000 or more. This gap between expectation and reality is the single biggest reason ADU projects become stressful, delayed, or abandoned, not because costs "got out of control," but because key expenses were never included in the first place. Most ADU cost failures happen before construction even begins, driven by incomplete information in one of the most expensive and tightly regulated construction environments in the country. Instead of relying on best-case scenarios, quick quotes, or marketing numbers, this book explains where ADU budgets actually fail—through hidden soft costs like design, engineering, permits, and energy reports;

site-specific conditions such as soil, slope, drainage, and utility distances that can dramatically affect foundations and infrastructure; and contractor pricing traps like low allowances, vague scopes, and change orders that quietly shift risk to the homeowner. The goal of this book is simple: to help you create a realistic, all-in ADU budget before you spend a dollar or sign a contract, so you can compare bids accurately, ask better questions, spot unrealistic estimates early, avoid expensive surprises, and make confident financial decisions. This is not a sales pitch, a promise of cheap construction, or a shortcut—it is a decision-making framework designed to replace optimism with clarity and give you control from the first planning conversation to the day you receive your Certificate of Occupancy. Your ADU may not be the cheapest one built, but it can be one of the most predictable, and in Southern California ADU construction, predictability is the real win.

PART I

THE ANATOMY OF ADU COSTS

CHAPTER 1

HARD COSTS VS. SOFT COSTS: THE CRITICAL DISTINCTION

Before you can create a realistic budget for your ADU, you need to understand a basic truth about construction costs: **not all costs are visible.**

Every ADU project is made up of two major categories of expenses:

- Hard Costs
- Soft Costs

Most homeowners focus almost entirely on Hard Costs because they are easy to see and easier to imagine. Unfortunately, this is also why budgets fall apart.

After reviewing hundreds of ADU estimates and completed projects across Southern California, one pattern appears again and again: homeowners' budget accurately for what they can see—and underestimate what they can't.

It is the **invisible Soft Costs** that are most often ignored, underestimated, or completely missing from early estimates. These costs are the **single biggest cause of budget shock.**

Hard Costs: The Physical Build

Hard Costs are the expenses required to physically construct the ADU. These are the costs that turn drawings into an actual building.

Think of Hard Costs **as everything you can touch.**

Hard Costs include:

- **Materials**: Lumber, concrete, roofing, drywall, windows, doors, electrical wiring, plumbing pipes, fixtures, cabinets, flooring, and finishes.
- **Labor**: The wages paid to the General Contractor and all subcontractors, such as framers, plumbers, electricians, roofers, drywall installers, and painters.
- **Equipment**: Dumpster rentals, scaffolding, heavy machinery, temporary power, and water hookups.

Once the design is finalized, Hard Costs are **relatively predictable.** They are closely tied to:

- The size of the ADU
- The complexity of the design
- The quality of finishes you choose

Hard Costs feel more predictable because they are based on visible scope: square footage, materials, and labor hours. This makes them easier to estimate—and easier to underestimate the total project cost.

Soft Costs: The Invisible Overhead

Soft Costs are the expenses required to **legally approve, design, finance, and manage** your ADU—but they do not become part of the physical structure.

You can't see Soft Costs when the ADU is finished, but you will absolutely feel them in your budget.

Soft Costs typically include:

- **Design and Engineering:** Architect fees, structural engineering, and Title 24 energy compliance consultants.
- **Permits and City Fees:** Plan check fees, building permits, school fees (when applicable), and utility connection charges.
- **Financing Costs:** Construction loan interest, appraisals, loan origination fees, and lender-required reports.
- **Insurance:** Builder's Risk insurance, General Liability insurance, and Workers' Compensation coverage.
- **Surveys and Technical Reports:** Soils reports, topographical surveys, tree reports, and other site-specific studies.

Many early ADU estimates exclude some or all Soft Costs. This doesn't mean the project is cheaper—it means the estimate is incomplete.

How Big Are Soft Costs, really?

While every project is different, a realistic rule of thumb for a **contractor-built ADU in Southern California** is this:

Soft Costs typically account for 15% to 25% of the total project budget.

If your total ADU budget is $300,000, Soft Costs alone may range from **$45,000 to $75,000.**

If an estimate doesn't clearly account for these costs, the missing money will surface later—often after you've already committed.

In real-world ADU projects, Soft Costs are rarely eliminated—they are simply delayed, disguised, or shifted to the homeowner later in the process.

The Typical Percentage Breakdown

While every project is unique, a common rule of thumb for a contractor-built ADU in Southern California is that Soft Costs will account for 15% to 25% of the total project budget.

Cost Category	Typical Percentage of Total Budget
Hard Costs	75% - 85%
Soft Costs	15% - 25%

If you budget $200,000 for your ADU, you must immediately allocate $30,000 to $50,000 for Soft Costs alone. Failing to account for this critical distinction is the first step toward a budget overrun. By budgeting for the "invisible" costs from the start, you establish a realistic financial foundation for your project.

Chapter Checklist: What You Should Understand Now

Before moving on, make sure the following are true:

- ☐ I understand the difference between Hard Costs and Soft Costs
- ☐ I know that Soft Costs do not reduce construction quality—they exist regardless
- ☐ I know that Soft Costs can represent up to one-quarter of my total budget

- [ ] I will not trust an ADU estimate that only focuses on construction costs

Do This Now: Immediate Actions

1. **Review any existing ADU estimate you have:** Highlight which line items are Hard Costs and which are Soft Costs.
2. **Ask where Soft Costs are listed:** If they are missing or vague, assume they are not fully included.
3. **Set aside a preliminary Soft Cost allowance:** Use 20% of your total target budget as a planning placeholder.
4. **Pause before "locking in" a number:** A low early estimate often means incomplete information, not savings.

Scripts & Questions You Can Use

Script: When Reviewing an Estimate

"Can you walk me through which costs are considered Hard Costs, and which are Soft Costs, and confirm that both are fully included in this total?"

Questions to Ask a Contractor or Designer

- "Which Soft Costs are not included in this number?"
- "Who is responsible for permit fees and utility connection charges?"
- "Does this estimate include insurance and construction loan interest?"

- "What Soft Costs have homeowners typically underestimated on past projects?"

Red-Flag Answer to Watch For

"Those costs usually come later."

That answer almost always means they **are not included**.

CHAPTER 2

THE PERMIT & FEE SHOCK: UTILITY CONNECTION CHARGES

Of all the Soft Costs in an ADU project, **city and utility fees are often the most surprising—and the most painful.**

These fees are:

- **Mandatory**
- **Non-negotiable**
- **Required before construction can begin**

They are charged by cities, counties, and utility companies simply for the right to build and connect your ADU to existing infrastructure.

After reviewing hundreds of ADU budgets, these fees are consistently the ones homeowners say they "never saw coming."

Because these costs can easily add tens of thousands of dollars to your project, they must be researched and included early, not discovered halfway through the process.

Plan Check and Building Permit Fees

Before your ADU can be built, the city or county must review your plans and approve the work. This review process is not free.

These fees typically include:

- **Plan Check Fees (Paid Upfront):** These cover the time city staff spend reviewing your plans. This may include planners, building officials, structural engineers, and fire department reviewers.

No plan review = no permit.

- **Building Permit Fees (Paid When the Permit Is Issued):** These fees cover the cost of inspections during construction, including:

o Foundation inspection

o Framing inspection

o Electrical and plumbing "rough-in" inspections

o Final inspection

In most jurisdictions, these fees are calculated based on:

- The **size** of the ADU
- The **estimated construction value**

Why These Fees Feel Arbitrary

Permit fees are not based on what your ADU costs you. They are based on what the city believes it will cost them to review and inspect it.

Impact Fees: Paying for Public Services

Impact fees are charges imposed by local agencies to offset the strain a new housing unit places on public infrastructure and services.

In simple terms, these fees exist because **more housing means more demand** on schools, parks, roads, and utilities.

Common impact fees include:

- **School District Fees:** Charged to help fund new or expanded schools due to population growth.
- **Park and Recreation Fees:** Used to create or maintain public parks and recreational facilities.

A Small Win for ADU Owners

California law has capped or eliminated some impact fees for ADUs under 750 square feet. However, larger ADUs may still be subject to significant charges.

Do not assume these fees don't apply to you—verify them.

Utility Connection Fees: The Biggest Wild Card

The largest and most unpredictable Soft Cost is often the fee for connecting your ADU to existing utility systems.

These costs vary widely depending on:

- Your city

- Your utility provider
- Whether a new connection or upgrade is required

Common utility-related fees include:

- **Sewer and Water Connection Fees:** If your ADU requires a new connection to the public sewer or water main, the utility company may charge a Capacity Fee or Connection Fee. These fees can be extremely high—especially for sewer—because they are meant to fund expansion of the public system.
- **Electricity and Gas:** Connecting to an existing service panel is usually less expensive. However, if your ADU requires:

o A new electrical meter

o A service upgrade

o A separate gas connection

the utility company will charge for the meter, labor, and any required infrastructure upgrades.

Why Utility Fees Cause Budget Shock

Utility fees are rarely included in early estimates because they depend on utility company decisions—not contractor pricing.

How to Get Fee Estimates Early (Before It's Too Late)

You do **not** need finalized plans to get rough estimates for these fees.

Taking these steps early can save you from a **$20,000–$50,000 surprise later.**

Step 1: Contact the Planning Department

Call your local city or county planning department and ask for:

- The ADU fee schedule
- Any written guidance on permit and impact fees

Step 2: Contact Utility Providers

Call your local:

- Water provider
- Sewer provider
- Electric company
- Gas company

Be prepared to share:

- Approximate ADU size
- Location on the property
- Whether the unit is detached or attached

Ask for:

- Capacity fees
- Connection charges
- Meter and service upgrade costs

Homeowners who investigate these fees early are far less likely to pause, redesign, or abandon their ADU project due to unexpected costs.

Chapter Checklist: What You Should Understand Now

- ☐ City and utility fees are mandatory and unavoidable
- ☐ Permit fees pay for plan review and inspections
- ☐ Impact fees may still apply depending on ADU size
- ☐ Utility connection fees are often the largest unknown
- ☐ These costs must be researched before finalizing a budget

Do This Now: Immediate Actions

1. **Request your city's ADU fee schedule:** Do not rely on estimates from third parties alone.
2. **Call utility providers directly:** Ask specifically about capacity fees and service upgrades.
3. **Document all estimates in writing:** Even ballpark numbers help prevent budget shock.
4. **Add a contingency line for utilities:** Utility costs often change after site review.

Scripts & Questions You Can Use

Script: When Talking to the City

"I'm planning an ADU and want to understand all permit, plan check, and impact fees that would apply before I move forward."

Script: When Calling Utility Companies

"I'm planning an ADU of approximately ___ square feet. Can you estimate any capacity fees, connection charges, or service upgrades that may be required?"

Questions to Ask

- "Will this ADU require a new sewer or water connection?"
- "Would a separate electrical meter be required?"
- "What fees are paid upfront versus later?"
- "What costs change after a site visit?"

Red-Flag Answer

"We'll know once construction starts."

That usually means the cost is real—but currently unknown.

CHAPTER 3

SITE-SPECIFIC COSTS: THE HIDDEN BUDGET KILLERS

A contractor can build the **exact same 800-square-foot ADU** on two different properties—and the final cost can vary by **$50,000 or more.**

This difference has nothing to do with the design or the contractor.

It has everything to do with the site.

After reviewing ADU projects across Southern California, site-specific conditions are one of the most common reasons early estimates fall apart.

Site-Specific Costs are determined by the unique physical characteristics of your property. These costs are often missing from early estimates because they are harder to see and harder to explain—but they are essential for building a realistic budget.

Soil: The Ground Beneath Your Budget

The soil under your ADU is one of the first—and most important—variables.

Soils Report (Soft Cost)

Most building departments require a soils report before approving construction.

A soils report is prepared by a geotechnical engineer and analyzes:

- Soil composition
- Load-bearing capacity
- How the soil reacts to moisture

This report is a Soft Cost and typically costs a few thousand dollars.

Foundation Design (Hard Cost Impact)

Once the soils report is complete, the structural engineer designs the foundation.

If the soil is:

- Expansive clay (swells when wet)
- Weak or unstable

then a simple concrete slab may not be allowed.

Instead, the engineer may require:

- Deep-drilled piers
- Reinforced grade beams

This can add **$10,000 to $30,000** to your **Hard Costs.**

Why Soil Gets Ignored Early

Soil problems don't show up on drawings or renderings—but they directly affect foundation cost. Ignoring soil conditions early almost always leads to redesigns and budget increases later.

Slope: The Cost of Making Land Flat

A flat lot is the cheapest scenario.

A sloped lot introduces significant additional costs.

Grading

Grading means moving earth to create a level area for construction.

The steeper the slope:

- The more soil must be moved
- The more complex the engineering

Grading costs rise quickly as slope increases.

Retaining Walls

If the slope is significant, retaining walls may be required to hold back soil.

These are structural elements, not landscaping features, and they require:

- Engineering
- Reinforced construction

Typical costs range from $100 to $300 per linear foot and can climb higher depending on height and soil conditions.

Drainage

Sloped lots require intentional drainage solutions to prevent water from collecting near the foundation.

This may include:

- French drains
- Swales
- Subsurface drainage systems

Each adds design complexity and cost.

Slopes Multiply Costs

Slopes don't just add one cost—they trigger grading, retaining, drainage, and engineering expenses at the same time.

Access: When Logistics Increase Labor Costs

Construction is not just about building—it's about moving people and materials.

If your lot is difficult to access, labor costs increase.

Tight Access

If the ADU is located in the backyard with only a narrow side yard:

- Large equipment can't be used
- Materials must be carried by hand

This increases labor time for:

- Framing
- Concrete

- Drywall
- Roofing
- Finishes

Limited Parking and Storage

If contractors cannot:

- Park trucks nearby
- Store materials on site

they spend more time transporting materials—time that shows up in your bid.

Labor Is Time-Based

When access slows the job down, labor costs rise—even if materials stay the same.

Utilities: The Distance Penalty

The farther your ADU is from existing utility connections, the more it will cost.

Trenching

Every foot of trenching for:

- Sewer
- Water
- Electrical
- Gas

adds cost.

Long utility runs from the main house to a detached ADU can add thousands of dollars to site preparation alone.

Sewage Ejector Pumps

If your ADU sits lower than the main sewer line, gravity won't work.

In this case, a sewage ejector pump is required to push waste uphill.

This adds:

- Equipment cost
- Installation cost
- Ongoing maintenance
- A potential failure point

Hidden Utility Complexity

Utility challenges often don't appear until site conditions are reviewed—long after early budgets are shared.

Site-related costs are rarely eliminated; they are usually discovered late—after design decisions are harder and more expensive to change.

Chapter Checklist: What You Should Understand Now

- ☐ Two identical ADUs can cost very different amounts based on site conditions
- ☐ Soil directly affects foundation design and cost

- ☐ Slopes trigger grading, retaining walls, and drainage expenses
- ☐ Limited access increases labor costs
- ☐ Long utility runs and elevation changes add significant hidden costs

Do This Now: Immediate Actions

1. **Ask whether a soils report will be required:** Do not assume your soil is "normal."
2. **Walk your property with access in mind:** Note tight side yards, slopes, and obstacles.
3. **Measure distances to utility connections:** Long runs = higher trenching costs.
4. **Flag elevation differences early:** Ask whether gravity sewer service is possible.

Scripts & Questions You Can Use Immediately

Script: When Talking to a Contractor

"What site conditions could increase the cost of this ADU, even if the design stays the same?"

Questions to Ask

- "Will this lot require a soils report?"
- "What foundation types might be required here?"
- "How does site access affect labor costs?"
- "How far will utilities need to be trenched?"

- "Would a sewage ejector pump be required?"

Red-Flag Answer

"We'll figure that out later."

That usually means **the cost exists—but isn't in the estimate yet.**

PART II

DECODING THE CONTRACTOR'S BID

CHAPTER 4

COMPARING BIDS: APPLES TO APPLES

Once you have approved—or nearly approved—plans, the next step is to request bids from **General Contractors (GCs)**.

This is one of the most critical moments in your ADU project.

A contractor's bid is not just a number.

It is a **promise of price**, based on a specific understanding of what they believe they are building.

The problem is this:

Most homeowners assume all bids mean the same thing. They almost never do.

In real ADU projects, budget failures at the construction phase usually trace back to incomplete or misleading bids—not bad intentions, but unclear scope.

A low bid can be a trap.

A high bid may simply be more honest.

Your goal is not to find the cheapest contractor.

Your goal is to make sure every contractor is bidding on the exact same work.

The Single Most Important Tool: A Detailed Scope of Work (SOW)

The most effective way to protect yourself during bidding is to provide **every contractor with the same, detailed Scope of Work (SOW)**.

Do not allow contractors to define the scope for you.

If they do, you are no longer comparing bids—you are comparing assumptions.

What Your Scope of Work Must Include

1. Explicitly Reference the Plans

Your SOW should clearly state:

"This bid must be based on the attached architectural and engineering plans."

This prevents contractors from:

- Ignoring structural details
- Making assumptions about missing information
- Pricing a simplified version of the project

2. Specify Materials (When known)

If you have already selected materials, list them clearly:

- Manufacturer
- Model number
- Finish

- Quantity

Examples:

- Windows
- Flooring
- Roofing material
- Cabinets

This removes guesswork and prevents **material downgrades disguised as "equivalents."**

3. Clearly Define Inclusions and Exclusions

Spell out what must be included, such as:

- City permit fees
- Dumpster rental
- Temporary utilities
- Final clean-up

Also clearly list what is excluded, such as:

- Landscaping
- Appliances
- Utility connection fees paid directly by the homeowner

A vague scope allows a contractor to appear cheaper by leaving things out. A detailed scope forces the real cost to show up early—when you can still make informed decisions.

Red Flags in a Low Bid

If one bid comes in more than 15–20% lower than the others,

treat it with caution.

In almost every case, it points to one of two problems:

1. Inexperience

The contractor may not fully understand:

- ADU permitting complexity
- Site conditions
- Utility requirements

This often leads to:

- Missed costs
- Delays
- Change orders later

2. Intentional Omissions

Some bids are low because key items are simply missing, such as:

- Utility trenching
- Permit fees
- Title 24 energy compliance
- Insurance costs

These costs don't disappear—they reappear later as change orders, when you have less leverage.

The Change Order Trap

A low bid often wins the job. Change orders are how the contractor makes the real money.

The Most Important Section of Any Bid: Exclusions

The **Exclusions** section tells you what the contractor is not doing.

This section matters more than the total price.

Example:

- **Bid A** excludes all city permit fees
- **Bid B** includes all city permit fees

Bid A is not cheaper—you are just paying part of the cost elsewhere.

If a critical item is missing from the bid:

- Assume it is excluded
- Ask for a written price to include it

Inconsistent exclusion lists are one of the most common reasons homeowners think bids are wildly different—when they're not.

How to Compare Bids Objectively (Without Guessing)

To compare bids fairly, create a Bid Comparison Matrix.

This removes emotion and focuses attention on scope, gaps, and risk.

Step 1: List Components Vertically

Examples:

- Site preparation

- Foundation
- Framing
- Roofing
- Electrical rough-in
- Plumbing rough-in
- Soft costs
- Allowances

Step 2: List Contractors Horizontally

Then fill in what each contractor included.

Sample Bid Comparison Matrix

Component	Contractor A	Contractor B	Contractor C	Notes
Soft Costs				
Permit Fees	Included	Excluded ($15k)	Included	
Hard Costs				
Foundation	$25,000	$20,000	$28,000	Bid B unusually low—verify rebar specs
Framing	$35,000	$38,000	$36,000	
Allowances				
Flooring	$2,000	$5,000	$3,500	Bid A allowance likely unrealistic
Total	$185,000	$195,000	$205,000	

Patterns will emerge quickly:

- Missing line items
- Unrealistic allowances
- Areas requiring clarification

You're not comparing prices. You're comparing assumptions, risk, and completeness.

Chapter Checklist: What You Should Understand Now

- ☐ A bid is only meaningful if the scope is identical
- ☐ Low bids often hide omissions or inexperience
- ☐ The Exclusions section matters more than the total price
- ☐ Allowances can distort bids significantly
- ☐ A comparison matrix reveals risk quickly

Do This Now: Immediate Actions

1. **Create a written Scope of Work:** Use it for every contractor—no exceptions.
2. **Request itemized bids:** Avoid lump-sum numbers with no breakdown.
3. **Highlight exclusions:** Compare them side by side.
4. **Normalize allowances:** Ask all contractors to use the same allowance values.

Scripts & Questions You Can Use Immediately

Script: When Requesting Bids

"I'm asking all contractors to bid based on the same plans and scope so I can make a fair comparison."

Questions to Ask Contractors

- "What assumptions did you make that are not shown on the plans?"
- "Which costs are excluded from this bid?"
- "Which items are allowances, and how were those numbers determined?"
- "What site conditions could trigger a change order?"

Red-Flag Answer

"We'll work that out as we go."

That usually means **the price is not final—and the risk is yours.**

CHAPTER 5

THE ALLOWANCE TRAP: HOW TO AVOID GETTING TRICKED

Allowances are one of the most common—and most effective—ways an ADU budget quietly grows after construction begins.

On paper, allowances look harmless. In reality, they are often used to **artificially lower a contractor's bid**, win the job, and then recover profit later through **change orders**.

In real ADU projects, allowances are one of the top reasons the final cost is tens of thousands of dollars higher than the contract price.

To protect yourself, you must understand **what allowances are, why they exist,** and how **to neutralize them before signing a contract.**

What an "Allowance" Really Means

An **Allowance** is a placeholder dollar amount included in the contract for a material or fixture that has not yet been selected.

Instead of pricing the real item, the contractor inserts a number and moves on.

Common allowance items include:

- Flooring (tile, wood, carpet)
- Light fixtures
- Plumbing fixtures (faucets, sinks, toilets)
- Appliances
- Cabinets and countertops

Here's how it works:

- The allowance amount is included in the contract total
- You make your actual selections later
- If the real cost is higher, you pay the difference
- If the real cost is lower, you receive a credit

> An allowance is not a price—it's a guess. And guesses are almost always low.

Why Contractors Use Allowances

Allowances are not automatically bad. They exist for practical reasons—but they are often abused.

Reason #1: Speed

Allowances allow contractors to submit bids without waiting for you to make every design decision.

That part is reasonable.

Reason #2: To Win the Bid

By setting allowances **unrealistically low,** a contractor can:

- Lower their total bid
- Appear more competitive
- Win the job

This is where allowances become dangerous.

A Common Example

- Kitchen cabinet allowance: **$1,000**
- Realistic, functional cabinets: **$5,000**

That $4,000 difference doesn't disappear.

It returns later—**plus markup.**

Most homeowners compare the total bid number—not the allowance assumptions hidden inside it.

The Change Order Trap

When your actual selection exceeds the allowance, the difference is added to your contract price as a **Change Order.**

And it doesn't stop there.

The contractor will also add:

- Overhead
- Profit markup (typically 15–25%)

Example:

- Allowance: $1,000
- Actual cost: $2,000
- Difference: $1,000

- Contractor markup (20%): $200

Total Change Order: $1,200

Multiply this across cabinets, flooring, fixtures, and appliances—and the budget damage adds up fast.

In completed ADU projects, allowance overruns are rarely surprises—they are predictable outcomes of unrealistic numbers.

How to Set Realistic Allowances (And Shut Down the Trap)

The best defense against allowance abuse is preparation before bidding is complete.

Step 1: Shop Early

Visit:

- Showrooms
- Online retailers
- Manufacturer websites

Choose realistic products—not luxury upgrades, but not bargain-basement items either.

Step 2: Get Real Prices

Obtain:

- Written quotes
- Screenshots with model numbers
- Vendor estimates

These numbers represent real market cost, not guesses.

Step 3: Force Realistic Allowances

Provide your selections and pricing to every contractor and say:

"Please use these actual costs as the allowances in your bid."

This locks the real cost into the contract upfront, where it belongs.

If a contractor refuses to use realistic allowances, they are signaling that they plan to make money later—through change orders.

Why This Matters More Than You Think

When allowances are realistic:

- The contract price reflects reality
- Profit is transparent
- Budget risk drops dramatically

When allowances are low:

- The contract price is fictional
- Profit is hidden
- Cost overruns are guaranteed

Chapter Checklist: What You Should Understand Now

☐ An allowance is a placeholder—not a real price

- ☐ Low allowances make bids look cheaper than they are
- ☐ Exceeding an allowance always triggers a change order
- ☐ Change orders include markup, not just material cost
- ☐ Realistic allowances must be set before signing a contract

Do This Now: Immediate Actions

1. **Identify every allowance in your bid:** Highlight them—these are risk zones.
2. **Compare allowance amounts across bids:** Big differences = misleading pricing.
3. **Price out your likely selections now:** Even rough realism is better than guessing.
4. **Normalize allowances across contractors:** Make everyone use the same numbers.

Scripts & Questions You Can Use Immediately

Script: When Reviewing a Bid

"These allowance amounts seem low. Can we adjust them to reflect realistic market pricing before finalizing the contract?"

Questions to Ask

- "What assumptions were used to set these allowances?"

- "What happens if my selections exceed the allowance?"
- "What markup is applied to allowance overruns?"
- "Can we revise the contract to reduce allowances?"

Red-Flag Answer

"Most people go over allowances—it's normal."

That usually means **the overage is built into their business model.**

Final Thought

By demanding realistic allowances upfront, you force honesty into the contract.

The goal is not to eliminate profit—it's to eliminate surprises.

CHAPTER 6

CHANGE ORDERS: THE CONTRACTOR'S PROFIT CENTER

A Change Order is a written agreement that modifies the original construction contract. In most cases, it results in:

- An increase in price
- An extension of the schedule

Some change orders are legitimate and unavoidable.

Many are not.

In completed ADU projects, change orders are the single most common reason the final cost exceeds the contract price.

Change orders are also the **primary mechanism** through which a low bid becomes a highly profitable project for a contractor.

Understanding **why change orders happen, which ones are justified,** and how to control them is essential to protecting your budget.

The Three Types of Change Orders (And Why They Matter)

Not all change orders are the same.

They fall into three clear categories, and each must be handled differently.

1. Owner-Driven Change Orders: The Cost of Changing Your Mind

Owner-driven change orders occur when **you request a change** after the contract is signed and construction is already underway.

These are the most common—and the most preventable.

Common Examples

- Changing flooring after installation has begun
- Moving walls after framing
- Upgrading fixtures after rough-in
- Swapping doors or windows mid-build

Example:

You decide you want a sliding glass door instead of a French door after the wall has already been framed.

What looks like a simple preference change now requires:

- Demolition
- New framing
- Possible structural review
- A new inspection

Why Timing Matters

The cost of changing something on paper is close to zero. The cost of changing it after construction begins includes labor, materials, delays, and inspections.

How to Minimize Owner-Driven Change Orders

- Finalize all design decisions before signing the contract
- Select materials early
- Avoid "we'll decide later" language

Indecision is not free—it is expensive.

2. Unforeseen Conditions: Legitimate Surprises

These change orders result from conditions that could not reasonably be known before construction began.

They are not the contractor's fault—and they are sometimes unavoidable.

Common Examples

- Hidden, abandoned septic tanks
- Unknown underground utilities
- Unstable soil discovered during excavation
- Unpermitted or unsafe existing construction

Example:

During site preparation, the crew discovers an old, unmapped septic tank that must be removed and the soil compacted before construction can continue.

Not Every Change Order Is a Scam

Some problems are literally buried. The key is not avoiding all change orders—it's managing them correctly.

How to Handle Unforeseen Conditions

Your contract should clearly state:

- How unforeseen conditions are defined
- How pricing is determined
- How schedule extensions are calculated

When one arises:

1. Demand **a written change order**
2. Review the scope, cost, and time impact
3. Ask questions before approving

You should also have the right to:

- Request documentation
- Seek a second opinion if costs seem excessive

Homeowners who treat unforeseen conditions calmly—but insist on documentation—avoid both overpaying and unnecessary conflict.

3. Contractor-Driven Change Orders: The Real Danger Zone

This is the most dangerous type of change order.

Contractor-driven change orders occur when a contractor claims:

- A required item was "not included"
- The work is "more complex than expected"
- The bid assumed something different

Often, this happens because the original contract was vague or incomplete.

A Common Example

The contractor claims the cost of a required fire sprinkler system was not included—even though the plans clearly show it.

This is not a surprise.

This is **a scope failure**.

Where Low Bids Come Back to Bite You

Many low bids rely on vague scope so missing items can be added later—at a premium.

How to Protect Yourself

1. Use a Detailed Scope of Work (SOW)

If an item is clearly included in the SOW:

- The contractor must perform it
- At the agreed-upon price

Ambiguity always favors the contractor.

2. Never Approve Verbal Changes

Never allow work to proceed based on:

- Verbal agreements
- Text messages
- "We'll sort it out later" promises

Every change must be documented.

3. Require a Written, Signed Change Order

A valid change order must include:

- A clear description of the new work
- The exact cost
- The schedule impact

Without this, you have no legal protection against surprise charges later.

The Golden Rule of Change Orders

No signature. No work. No exceptions.

Chapter Checklist: What You Should Understand Now

- ☐ Change orders usually increase cost and time
- ☐ Owner-driven changes are the most preventable
- ☐ Unforeseen conditions must be documented
- ☐ Contractor-driven change orders are the biggest risk
- ☐ Verbal agreements offer zero protection

Do This Now: Immediate Actions

1. **Review your contract for change-order language:** If it's vague, revise it before signing.
2. **Eliminate undecided selections:** Fewer decisions during construction = fewer change orders.

3. **Create a "no verbal changes" rule:** Apply it consistently.
4. **Track every approved change order:** Maintain a running total of added cost and time.

Scripts & Questions You Can Use Immediately

Script: When a Change Is Proposed

"Please provide a written change order detailing the scope, cost, and schedule impact before proceeding."

Questions to Ask

- "Is this change driven by my request, site conditions, or scope gaps?"
- "Where is this item addressed in the plans or Scope of Work?"
- "Can you break down the pricing for this change?"
- "Is there an alternative solution with less cost impact?"

Red-Flag Statement

"We'll just take care of it and adjust later."

That usually means **you're about to lose leverage.**

Final Thought

Change orders are not inherently bad.

Uncontrolled change orders are.

By locking down decisions early, insisting on clarity, and requiring written documentation, you prevent change orders from becoming the contractor's profit engine—and keep your budget grounded in reality.

PART III

BUDGETING AND FINANCIAL PROTECTION

CHAPTER 7

THE CONTINGENCY FUND: YOUR FINANCIAL SAFETY NET

No matter how detailed your plans are, how accurate your bids appear, or how trustworthy your contractor is, **every construction project encounters unexpected costs.**

This is not a failure of planning.

It is a reality of building.

Across completed ADU projects, unexpected costs are not the exception—they are the rule.

The difference between a **successful project** and a **financially stressful one** is not whether surprises happen, but whether you are prepared to absorb them.

That is why the **Contingency Fund** is the single most important line item in your entire ADU budget.

What a Contingency Fund Is (And What It Is Not)

A **Contingency Fund** is a dedicated pool of money set aside only for unexpected, unavoidable costs that arise during construction.

It is:

- Planned in advance
- Kept separate from your main budget
- Used sparingly and intentionally

It is not extra money for upgrades, preferences, or impulse decisions.

If you don't plan for surprises, the project will plan them for you—at the worst possible time.

The Rule of Thumb: 10–15% of Total Hard Costs

The industry standard recommendation for residential construction is to budget 10% to 15% of total Hard Costs as contingency.

Example:

- Contractor's Hard Cost bid: $250,000
- Recommended contingency:
    - 10% = $25,000
    - 15% = $37,500

This money should be:

- Liquid and accessible
- Not part of your everyday spending
- Not mentally "pre-spent"

It is your financial shock absorber—designed to prevent you from:

- Stopping construction mid-project

- Taking out high-interest loans
- Cutting quality to stay afloat

Projects without a contingency fund don't save money—they shift stress, delay decisions, and force compromises later.

When the Contingency Fund Should Be Used

The contingency fund is reserved for true emergencies and unavoidable costs—not preferences.

Appropriate Uses

- Unforeseen site conditions: (e.g., discovering an old oil tank or buried debris)
- Inspection failures requiring corrective work: (e.g., re-pouring part of a foundation)
- Sudden material price spikes due to supply issues
- Required utility upgrades not identified early

When the Contingency Fund Should Not Be Used

Using contingency for non-emergencies defeats its purpose.

Inappropriate Uses

- Upgrading finishes or materials
- Adding features not in the original plans
- Covering allowance overruns caused by unrealistic numbers

- Paying for contractor mistakes that should be covered by insurance

The contingency fund only works if you protect it. Once it's gone, every new issue becomes a crisis.

How to Manage the Contingency Fund Correctly

Every dollar spent from contingency should meet three conditions:

1. **It was not reasonably foreseeable**
2. **It is required to move the project forward**
3. **It is documented and approved by you**

This keeps the fund from slowly turning into a general slush account.

The Psychological Power of a Safety Net

Beyond finances, the contingency fund offers something just as valuable: **calm**.

When a problem inevitably arises—and it will—you won't panic.

You won't rush decisions.

You won't accept bad solutions just to keep moving.

Homeowners with a contingency fund make clearer decisions, resolve problems faster, and experience far less stress during construction.

This clarity prevents:

- Emotional decision-making

- Costly delays
- Escalating conflict

Think of the contingency fund as the price you pay for peace of mind during one of the most complex projects you'll ever manage.

Chapter Checklist: What You Should Understand Now

❒ Unexpected costs are unavoidable in construction

❒ A contingency fund protects both budget and momentum

❒ 10–15% of Hard Costs is the standard range

❒ Contingency is for emergencies—not upgrades

❒ Discipline determines whether the fund works

Immediate Actions

1. **Calculate your contingency fund today:** Base it on Hard Costs—not the total project.
2. **Separate the money mentally and financially:** Treat it as unavailable unless truly needed.
3. **Define contingency rules in writing:** Decide in advance what qualifies.
4. **Track every contingency expense:** Maintain transparency and control.

Scripts & Questions You Can Use Immediately

Script: When Reviewing Your Budget

"This contingency fund is reserved for unforeseen, unavoidable costs—not design upgrades or preferences."

Questions to Ask

- "Is this issue truly unforeseeable?"
- "Is this cost required to pass inspection or proceed?"
- "Is there a lower-cost solution that still meets code?"
- "Does this expense belong to contingency—or somewhere else?"

Red-Flag Statement

"We'll just pull it from contingency—it's fine."

That usually means **discipline is already slipping.**

Final Thought

You don't create a contingency fund because you expect problems.

You create it because you respect reality.

Handled correctly, the contingency fund keeps your ADU project **moving forward, financially stable, and emotionally manageable**—even when the unexpected shows up.

CHAPTER 8

PAYMENT SCHEDULES AND LIEN RELEASES

Your contract with your General Contractor (GC) will include a **payment schedule**—a plan that defines **when** you pay and **how much** you pay at each stage of construction.

This schedule is not administrative paperwork.

It is one of the **most powerful control tools** you have.

In ADU projects that go off the rails, the problem is rarely the total price—it's when the money was released.

A poorly structured payment schedule can leave you:

- With too much money paid and too little work completed
- Unable to motivate the contractor to finish
- Exposed to **mechanic's liens** on your property

A well-structured schedule protects your cash, your leverage, and your timeline.

California's 10% Down Payment Rule (Your First Line of Protection)

California law limits how much a contractor can request as a down payment.

A contractor may not ask for more than:

- **10% of the total contract price, or**
- **$1,000,**

  whichever is less

This rule exists for one reason:

> to prevent a contractor from collecting a large upfront payment and then walking away.

If a contractor asks for more than the legal down payment, that is not a misunderstanding—it is a red flag.

Progress Payments Must Be Earned—Not Promised

After the down payment, the remaining contract price should be paid in **progress payments.**

These payments must be tied to:

- **Clearly defined construction milestones**
- **Work that is fully completed**
- **City inspections that have passed**

Never release money based on:

- Calendar dates
- Percentages claimed by the contractor
- Statements like "we're basically done"

The Golden Rule of Payments:

Never pay for work that has not passed inspection.

What a Proper Payment Schedule Looks Like

Below is a typical milestone-based payment structure for an ADU project:

Milestone	Payment Trigger
Start	Contract signed (legal down payment only)
Foundation	Forms set, rebar inspected, concrete poured
Framing	Framing complete and passed Framing Inspection
Rough-In	Plumbing, electrical, and HVAC rough ins complete and passed inspection
Drywall	Drywall hung, taped, and finished
Final	Project complete and Certificate of Occupancy (C of O) issued

Why the Final Payment Matters Most

The **final payment should be the largest payment.**

It should **never** be released until:

- All work is complete
- All inspections have passed
- The city issues the Certificate of Occupancy (C of O)

This gives you maximum leverage to ensure:

- Punch-list items are completed
- The site is clean

- All loose ends are resolved

Projects that stall near the finish line almost always do so because the contractor has already been paid too much.

Mechanic's Liens: The Risk Most Homeowners Don't See Coming

A Mechanic's Lien is a legal claim placed on your property by:

- Contractors
- Subcontractors
- Material suppliers

It can be filed if they claim they were not paid—even if you paid the General Contractor.

A lien can:

- Block a home sale
- Prevent refinancing
- Require legal action to remove

The Harsh Reality

You can pay your GC in full—and still end up with a lien if subs or suppliers weren't paid.

Lien Releases: Your Only Real Protection

The only reliable way to protect yourself is to require Lien Releases with every payment.

There are two types—and you need both.

Conditional Lien Release (Before You Pay)

This document states:

> "Upon receipt of this payment, the signer will release their right to file a lien for the work covered."

You must receive this before issuing any payment.

Unconditional Lien Release (After the Check Clears)

This document states:

> "The signer has been paid and permanently waives their right to file a lien for the work covered."

You must receive this after the payment clears.

Final Payment Protection

Before issuing the **final payment,** you must collect:

- **Unconditional Final Lien Release from the General Contractor**
- **Unconditional Final Lien Releases from all major subcontractors and suppliers**

This is your last—and strongest—layer of protection.

No Releases, No Money

Lien releases are not optional paperwork. They are payment conditions.

Chapter Checklist: What You Should Understand Now

- ☐ Payment schedules control progress and leverage
- ☐ California law limits down payments
- ☐ Progress payments must align with inspections
- ☐ The final payment should be the largest
- ☐ Lien releases are essential for every payment

Do This Now: Immediate Actions

1. **Review your payment schedule carefully:** Confirm payments align with inspections—not dates.
2. **Cap the down payment at the legal limit:** No exceptions.
3. **Require lien releases with every payment:** Make it non-negotiable.
4. **Hold firm on the final payment:** No C of O = no final check.

Scripts & Questions You Can Use Immediately

Script: When Reviewing the Contract

"All payments will be tied to completed work that has passed inspection, and lien releases will be required with each payment."

Questions to Ask

- "Which inspection must pass before this payment is due?"
- "Who provides lien releases—GC only, or subs and suppliers as well?"
- "What documentation is required before final payment?"

Red-Flag Statement

"We don't usually do lien releases—it slows things down."

That usually means **your risk is being prioritized over their convenience.**

Final Thought

A payment schedule is not about mistrust.

It's about alignment.

When money flows in step with progress, everyone stays motivated, protected, and accountable—and your ADU project is far more likely to finish **on time, on budget, and without legal headaches.**

CHAPTER 9

TRACKING COSTS: THE SIMPLE SPREADSHEET

The difference between **a successful ADU budget and a runaway budget** is not luck.

It is a **simple, disciplined system** for tracking every dollar spent.

As the homeowner, you must maintain a **Budget vs. Actual spreadsheet** and update it **weekly**. This system is not about accounting—it is your **early warning system.**

In real ADU projects, budgets don't fail suddenly. They fail quietly, one unchecked expense at a time.

If you wait until the end of the project to "see where you landed," you've already lost control.

What "Budget vs. Actual" Really Means

A Budget vs. Actual spreadsheet compares:

- What you **planned** to spend
- What you **actually** spent
- The **difference** between the two

This comparison tells you where problems are forming, while you still have time to respond.

You can't control what you don't measure. Tracking weekly turns surprises into manageable decisions instead of emergencies.

How to Set Up Your Budget vs. Actual Spreadsheet

Your spreadsheet should **mirror the structure of your project,** not just list random expenses.

Organize it the same way your contractor's bid and your Soft Cost estimates are organized.

Required Columns

Your spreadsheet should include at least these columns:

- **Category**
- **Budgeted Amount**
- **Actual Cost**
- **Difference (Variance)**
- **Notes**

The Most Important Column

The "Difference" (Variance) column tells you the truth. Positive is good. Negative means action is required.

Sample Budget vs. Actual Table

Category	Budgeted Amount	Actual Cost	Difference (Variance)	Notes
Soft Costs				
Permits & Fees	$15,000	$16,500	–$1,500	Utility connection fee higher than expected
Hard Costs				
Foundation	$25,000	$24,500	+$500	Small discount for early payment
Framing	$35,000	$35,000	$0	
Allowances				
Flooring	$4,000	$5,200	–$1,200	Upgraded to higher-end LVP
Contingency	$25,000	$23,500	+$1,500	Remaining balance

Why Weekly Updates Are Non-Negotiable

The power of this system is **frequency**.

Updating monthly is too late.

Updating at the end is useless.

You must update the spreadsheet **at least once a week.**

Weekly Tracking Process

1. Review Every Invoice Immediately

- Enter every invoice and payment into the Actual Cost column

- Do not rely on memory or bank statements later

2. Watch the Variance

- Calculate the difference between budgeted and actual cost
- A negative number means you are over budget in that category

3. Take Action Early

If one category goes over budget, you still have choices elsewhere.

Example:

If flooring exceeds the budget by $1,200, you may decide to:

- Choose a more modest light fixture
- Reduce a finish allowance elsewhere
- Protect the contingency fund

This is how **small corrections prevent big overruns.**

Homeowners who track weekly almost always stay closer to their original budget than those who “check in later.”

Why Record-Keeping Matters After Construction Is Over

Your spreadsheet isn’t just for construction—it has long-term financial value.

1. Your Cost Basis (Tax Impact)

The total **Actual Cost** of your ADU becomes its **Cost Basis.**

This number is used by your accountant to calculate:

- Depreciation (if you rent the ADU)
- Capital gains (if you sell the property)

A **higher, well-documented cost basis** can mean **lower taxes** over time.

2. Appraisal Support (Value Impact)

Detailed records of:

- Materials
- Fixtures
- Professional services

help justify a **higher appraisal value** for your ADU.

This matters when:

- Refinancing
- Selling
- Leveraging equity

Paperwork Is Profit

A well-documented project doesn't just cost more—it proves why it's worth more.

Chapter Checklist: What You Should Understand Now

- ☐ Budget tracking is a control system, not bookkeeping
- ☐ Weekly updates prevent small overruns from compounding
- ☐ Variance is the key metric to watch

- ☐ Overspending in one area requires correction elsewhere
- ☐ Records increase tax efficiency and appraisal value

Do This Now: Immediate Actions

1. **Create your Budget vs. Actual spreadsheet today:** Do not wait until construction starts.
2. **Match it to your bid structure:** Consistency makes problems visible.
3. **Schedule a weekly review:** Put it on your calendar.
4. **Save every invoice and receipt:** Digital folders work well.

Scripts & Questions You Can Use Immediately

Script: For Yourself (Weekly Review)

"Where am I over budget, and what decision can I make now to correct it?"

Questions to Ask

- "Is this overage unavoidable or optional?"
- "Does this expense belong in contingency?"
- "What category can absorb this cost?"
- "Will this increase long-term value?"

Red-Flag Thought

"I'll catch up on this later."

That's how budgets quietly slip away.

Final Thought

Your Budget vs. Actual spreadsheet is not busywork.

It is **financial awareness in real time.**

Used correctly, it gives you control, clarity, and confidence—and ensures your ADU's financial story is accurate, defensible, and profitable long after construction is complete.

CONCLUSION

You have now built something far more important than an ADU—you've built financial clarity.

Where most homeowners rely on incomplete estimates and optimism, you now understand how ADU costs actually work. You know that a real budget is not a single number, but a structure—one that includes hard costs, soft costs, site-specific realities, and a contingency fund. Because of this, you are no longer vulnerable to the most common and costly mistakes.

This knowledge changes everything.

You can identify gaps before they become expenses, question numbers that don't reflect reality, and make decisions based on full project cost—not assumptions. That alone places you ahead of the majority of homeowners, many of whom only discover these truths after their budget has already been stretched.

But the real advantage is not just avoiding problems—it's gaining control.

You are no longer approaching your ADU as a hopeful homeowner. You are operating as an informed client—someone who understands how construction projects function, where risk hides, and how financial discipline directly impacts outcomes. That shift gives you leverage, confidence, and stability throughout the entire process.

And when that process is managed well, the results compound.

A well-structured ADU project delivers cost certainty, stronger equity, and a higher return on investment. Every dollar works with intention. Every decision supports long-term value. Instead of reacting to surprises, you move forward with clarity.

Because the goal was never to build the cheapest ADU.

The goal was to build the right one—without financial regret.

Now, with your Certificate of Occupancy issued, the transition is complete. This is no longer a project waiting for approval. It is a legal, insurable, income-producing asset. You are no longer navigating permits and uncertainty—you are managing something of lasting value.

The system that once felt complex now works in your favor.

Your ADU is not just finished—it is defensible, functional, and positioned to serve its purpose, whether that is generating income, supporting family, or increasing the long-term strength of your property.

Clarity got you here. Discipline sustained you.

And both will continue to serve you long after the build itself is complete.

You didn't just complete a project.

You built it the right way

Made in United States
Troutdale, OR
11/03/2026

56844685R00050

Contents

Once again I dedicate this book to my amazing husband, Sam, who is always there for us. Thank you for proof reading this book and providing a sounding board. And of course, thank you to my beautiful girls who both challenge and inspire me every single day.

Your FREE Budget Planner Bundle

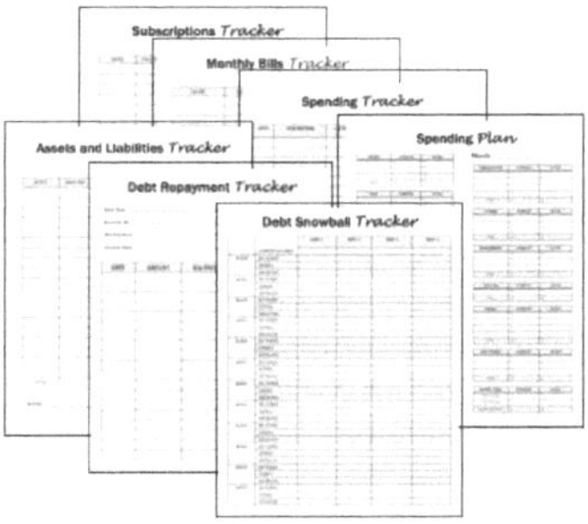

Take the guesswork out of where your money is going and start planning how to make it work for you

The Budget Planner Bundle is a set of templates to help you work out your current financial position, track your spending, put together a budget/spending plan and pay down debts

- Designed to be used while reading this book
- Choose from color or black and white templates
- Can be printed on US letter size or A4 size paper.

Download your free Budget Planner Bundle and start managing your money the smart way today. Go to www.zoemadden.com

Introduction

Everyone should be financially independent, but I believe this is even more of a necessity for women. Whether you are happily married or single, knowing how to control your money and make it work for you, instead of just working for it, is essential for life satisfaction. Unfortunately, many women never realize how dependent they are on the 'man' of the house—until the unforeseen occurs.

Samantha and her partner, Jacob, have been together for 20 years and have a ten-year-old girl together. Samantha thought their relationship was happy and secure. When she first got pregnant, they decided she would stay home to take care of the baby while Jacob worked and took care of the expenses. As their daughter grew, Samantha noticed Jacob becoming more distant. They fought continuously about the bills. Samantha had agreed to a small allowance to cover necessities for their daughter and the home, and rarely asked for anything more. One day Jacob didn't return from work. Instead he sent a text message saying he had met someone else. Samantha was devastated. On top of the grief and anger she had to work through, she realized she had no clue how to manage the bills for the home because she didn't even know what needed to be paid. The home was also in Jacob's name, so staying there was not an option long-term.

It's not a situation any of us want to consider finding ourselves in. But even if your relationship is solid, there are other events that can leave you taking on all the financial responsibilities. Health issues, disability, substance abuse and mental health issues can all impact the family income and can happen to anyone at any time. Being financially independent as a woman allows you to prepare for unexpected emergencies and tragedies.

Financial independence also impacts how we view ourselves as parents, partners, and caregivers, and not having an income adds uncertainty and stress to our lives. When the unexpected does happen, it can derail you and take years to learn how to get back on your feet.

Consider also that many families struggle to earn enough to meet the rising costs of living. Owning a home, raising children, preparing for the cost of their education, and all the other obligations of being an adult, require an impressive income. Often a single income home doesn't cover everything. A second income from you, the woman, not only lets you obtain financial independence but helps you contribute to the family. It provides the household a way to set and reach financial goals, even when inflation drives up the cost of living.

Being dependent on someone else to cover the bills and other expenses can lead to you feeling less worthy and confident. You may have aspirations and dreams, but don't feel you have the freedom to chase after them because you can't do it without someone else's financial support.

Teaching women how to achieve financial independence is something that I'm passionate about. It's a passion that grew during my time working as a professional financial planner. I've seen what can happen when women rely too much on a partner and leave all the financial decisions to them. Even worse, women often don't consider whose name the family assets are in. If the family home is only in the main breadwinner's name, this can leave the other party in a precarious financial situation.

Despite a lifetime of loyally bringing up the children, plus cooking and cleaning up after their spouse, women in this position can literally find themselves homeless after a nasty divorce or the loss of their spouse. If these women had been advised to maintain their financial independence throughout their marriage, they would have been far more able to get back on their feet after such a tragedy.

According to the U.S. Department of Housing and Urban Development, families with children account for about 30 percent of homeless people. Even more disturbing is the fact that the typical homeless family comprises a single mother with her two young children.

Now this may not be the path that you are on. You might be happily married, or young and still have the option to turn to your parents for financial assistance if anything should happen. But it doesn't matter what stage of life you are at. At some point, you are going to be responsible for your own finances, and if you don't understand what that entails before it happens, you may find yourself with far less than you have now.

Take, for instance, Anna. She's been happily married for 35 years. She and her husband have lived a comfortable life. They have two boys, both in their late teens. One is about to go off to college, and the other will follow in two years. As teens no longer need her to be their caregiver. They're capable of managing their own lives. Both have jobs, participate in various school activities, can drive themselves around, and do not rely on her for many of their basic needs. While Anna and her husband have followed a solid financial plan all these years and have set aside money for both boys to attend college, she has been feeling less valued. Although her husband makes enough to provide for both of them, Anna wants to return to the workforce because she needs something to make herself feel better about her capabilities. She's realized that once her children are gone, she will need something to work toward and would love to contribute financially to her and her husband's future goals. For years she's put her professional aspirations on hold because she felt bad about asking her husband to support these goals with his income. While she was happy to stay home and care for her children when it was necessary, she wants to find herself again.

It's not uncommon for women to experience a lack of self-worth because they are not earning or contributing financially to their household. On top of that, if you feel unable to manage household expenses, or even your own money, this doesn't feel like a great place to be in. It can put you in a position of feeling less than, instead of equal to, your partner.

Obtaining financial independence is one simple way you can regain your self-worth, manage life's trials and tribulations, feel more secure, and relieve the pressure on your partner to manage the financial burdens themselves. With financial independence, you feel as though you have more control over your life and choices. With this independence, you also gain the empowering feeling of knowing you are setting a good example for your children and can feel confident about teaching them how to handle their own money.

This book is designed to motivate you to take control of your destiny and create opportunities for yourself. This doesn't mean that the role of your partner is any less significant or that your relationship is heading towards the rocks. You will learn that when you feel more financially secure and capable in your relationship, both you and your partner can achieve greater success. Things that once seemed impossible, like week-long family vacations, a new home, or even early retirement, come within reach.

The information in this book will provide you with a greater understanding of the importance of financial independence. You will learn how to track spending, budget, get rid of debt, and make financial goals for your future. You can start to feel excited about what is possible for you and your family's life. Most importantly, you will feel more secure and prepared for any crisis that you find yourself facing.

It's my wish that by the end of this book, you will have a clear understanding of what financial independence means and begin to take action to achieve it. This book will provide you with many suggestions to help you achieve financial independence while also being able to plan for your future. You can also download some free templates from my website www.zoemadden.com. These useful resources will help you get your finances under control and include:

- Assets and Liabilities Inventory
- Subscriptions Tracker
- Monthly Bills
- Spending Tracker
- Spending Plan
- Debt Payoff Tracker
- Debt Snowball worksheet.

Please note that I've referred to the traditional terms of husband and wife throughout this book. However, the sentiment and strategies apply equally to same sex relationships where one party may earn more than the other and/or where one party stays home to care for children while the other works to support the family.

I also want to add that, as important as money is, we shouldn't place more importance on it than the most precious commodities we have – namely our time, our health and our relationships. Throughout your journey to financial independence don't forget to take the time to care for your health so you have the energy to take care of others and what truly matters to you. Check out my first book, *Stop Putting Yourself Last: The Self-Care Book For Moms* to help you practice self-care no matter how short of time you are.

Right, let's begin!

Important Legal Note

The information provided in this book does not take into consideration your personal financial situation and is generally factual in nature. Please consider it to be general life advice for educational purposes only and does not constitute financial advice nor financial product advice in any way. Before acting, you should consider seeking independent personal financial advice that is tailored to your needs from an appropriately licensed or authorised financial adviser.

Chapter 1

The History of Women and Finances

"I have yet to hear a man ask for advice on how to combine marriage and a career."
– Gloria Steinem

Marriage, domestic roles, and the workplace look a lot different to how they looked in the 1800s and 1900s. Women used to be seen but not heard. Imagine that if you can! Men were dominant in every aspect of the world, but slowly this shifted. The shift started some time ago, but it's still a work in progress. While women are no longer considered property and don't need a man's consent to open a bank account or create a personal income, we're still struggling to be viewed as financially competent and deserving. The role of women, being the housewife and maintaining the home, is one that many women still fight to break away from. Today, women have a much louder say in handling their money, but the social labels and views women have been carrying around are still an issue.

I think it's important to understand the traditional gender roles women had to abide by. It gives us an insight on why many women shy away from managing household income and let their spouses maintain much of the control over income and spending. Many women still prefer to stay home and take care of the kids, either because they want to or because child care costs are absurd and they have to. But, whether you choose to work in the home taking care of the kids or outside the home, many women unconsciously have the mindset that their partners should make the majority of financial decisions.

Generations of women have had to rely on their spouses for financial support and understanding. It was not so long ago that women began to embrace their financial independence and how important it was for them to know and take part in the cash flow of the home. Unfortunately, the societal views and restrictions women faced in the past are not long forgotten and still influence the role a woman plays in her personal finances after marriage or while in a relationship.

Introducing my heroine, Hetty Green

Henrietta Howland Robinson (Hetty Green), infamously known as the "Wizard of Finance," may have been one of the first women to proclaim the need for women and young girls to understand and have control over their own finances. She was also an impeccable role model and proof that women were more than capable of handling their own financial affairs and more.

Hetty Green was born in 1934 in New Bedford, Massachusetts. She came from a wealthy family. Her father owned one of the largest whaling fleets in their city and also made many profitable business moves throughout his life. Hetty first learned about stocks and business from her grandfather. By the time Hetty was 13, she was doing much of her family's bookkeeping and would accompany her father to many business meetings. It was from her father that Hetty gained an interest in finances and making money.

Her father died in 1865 and left Hetty with six million dollars of assets that ranged from cash to a warehouse and a trust fund. Because she was a woman, however, she had little control over any of the principal investments. She was able to use the interest from the trust to make many profitable investment moves. She mimicked what she learned from her father and invested in bonds with high returns, real estate, and other stocks. She was also smart about her investments and knew her best option for the biggest returns was to buy when something was low and not in demand and wait for the perfect timing to sell. She had no worries about holding on to stocks for much longer than most of her male counterpart investors chose to, and this paid off significantly. She would only sell when the price went up and there were plenty of buyers to sell to.

In 1867, Hetty married Edward Henry Green, but before she married him, she made him renounce his rights to her money. Smart lady! Shortly after they were married, they moved to London, and at the time, Hetty's annual profits from her investments totaled around $1.25 million. Her husband did not have the same investing sense as Hetty. He frequently suffered from losses in the stock market and made poor business moves. Luckily for him, Hetty was there to bail him out with her growing wealth.

At one point, she was trying to transfer nearly 26 million dollars of assets from one bank to another that she had partnered with. The bank she was trying to transfer from denied the transfer because her husband had a debt of over $700,000. Hetty eventually paid off his debt so she could transfer the assets, but it was an event that she never let him forget.

Despite the setbacks she encountered with her husband's financial affairs, Hetty continued to make smart investment moves. At the time of her death in 1916, Hetty was considered one of the richest women in the world, with a net worth at the time between $100 and $200 million. Today that would be closer to four billion dollars.

Keep in mind that what made Hetty Green such an inspiring and intriguing woman is that she was able to build her own wealth at a time where women were not even allowed to have bank accounts of their own. She was able to maintain control over her fortune throughout her life.

Even though she was fortunate enough to be born into wealth and had a great advantage thanks to the male figures that allowed her to learn and educate herself on money matters, it was still a time when women had little ownership over financial choices. At the time, women were just beginning to gain financial independence. They were allowed to receive an inheritance and own property but making investments was something that was new and still taboo throughout Hetty's life. What a gal is all I can say.

The Traditional Role of Women in the Home

Women are expected to take on many roles in the home, from being a good wife and mother to a maid, chef, teacher, and servant. Throughout history, women were considered property, not equal, and certainly not superior to men. Young women were controlled by their fathers until they were handed over to a husband, along with a dowry.

Even when marriage became a choice for women instead of a forced business transaction, they still had little freedom. For thousands of years, women were subservient to men, even if some parts of history contradicted this. A shift made women the child bearers and the men the decision-makers.

But, when required, such as during times of war, women had to take on men's roles in the work field and still maintain a home. When the men came back from the war, women were forced to return to domestic life. Women, however, have always made contributions to the family finances. Whether actively working in labor-intensive fields or secretly sewing for a small stipend, women have contributed financially, yet very few understood where or what the money was going toward.

This is seen throughout history and still today. The home is divided. Men take on certain responsibilities, and women take on another set. In ancient times, it was the men who went out to hunt, build, and find work. Women stayed home to cook, clean, and care for the children. This isn't so different from how many homes are organized today. Most times, neither parties in a marriage understand or have little input on the responsibilities other than their own.

If a man decides to stay home and care for the children while his wife works, some people may wonder how his wife can make enough to support their family. If a woman stays home to care for the children, there is no question about the family's finances. It's often just accepted that her husband makes enough and manages the financial affairs.

But many of us have a need and desire for financial independence, whether we stay home with the kids or continue to work. And with the cost of living now, it's often not possible for us to stay home with younger children, as the extra income is needed to support the home.

Why Women Struggle More Than Men

While history shows us that society has placed restrictions on a woman's financial independence, several factors contribute to insecurities around money today. While some of these issues are improving, we're often at an unfair disadvantage, making it completely understandable as to why women take on fewer financial responsibilities in the home.

Pay Gap

It's no secret that women today, still earn less than men. In nearly every industry, you will find women receiving a smaller paycheck than men in the same position. These women are working the same hours and have the same responsibilities. Even if a woman has more experience, she is still less likely to be offered the same pay as a man who has less. This has been an issue since the early 1860s when Susan B. Anthony and Elizabeth Cady Stanton began to advocate for men and women, regardless of color, to be paid equally for the work they performed. While they were able to give women the right to vote, the pay gap was very present.

In the 1940s, one of the first bills that rallied for equal pay in the workplace was presented, but it never even made it through to Congress. It would take another two decades for a bill that addressed the wage difference between men and women to get a vote. In 1963, the Equal Pay Act required employers to pay men and women the same as long as the job position required the same skills and effort and had the same responsibilities. But the act was flawed and allowed for many loopholes and different pay structures to come into play, where those of seniority were able to receive higher pay. Afterwards, women still made only 60 percent of what their male coworkers were making (Daugherty, 2021).

Unfortunately, for the rest of the 1900s, little progress was made on shrinking the wage gap. Even jobs that were essential for society, in which women primarily held positions, like teaching, the pay they received was far less than positions held by men in other industries. A woman's career was simply not valued as much as a position held by men. There was no urgency to provide women the same pay as men until 2007.

In 2007, one of the first cases of a woman suing their employer for unfair wages made headlines. The case *Ledbetter v. Goodyear Tire and Rubber Co.* had originally awarded Lilly Ledbetter, who worked for Goodyear, 3.5 million dollars for being underpaid for 19 years. The case was appealed and overturned, stating that Ledbetter missed her opportunity to file the wage discrimination, as the law at the time required individuals to make a claim within 180 days of when the discrimination first occurred. Based on these considerations, the ruling was reversed. However, because of this case, the Lilly Ledbetter Fair Pay Act was passed in 2009, which allowed for a long filing period for pay discrimination claims.

Since then, an ongoing fight for equal pay in the work field continues, despite more and more women joining the workforce. The Paycheck Fairness Act, which was first introduced in 2009, places a greater need to enforce fair pay rates for all individuals. It suggests increasing penalties for employers and businesses that violate anti-discrimination laws. Unfortunately, even after 10 years, the act has failed to make it all the way through Congress, and has been rejected by the Senate several times.

Despite the progress, here we are, over a hundred years later, and women are still fighting to make as much as men in the world. As of 2018, women were making 82 cents for every dollar a man in the same position makes (Daugherty, 2021). This is a mere 22 percent raise in a hundred years.

Unfortunately, this pay gap affects women of different races more significantly. African American women make 61 cents, and Hispanic or Latino women only make 53 cents for every dollar a man makes in the same position (Daugherty, 2021). This has been an ongoing struggle for women for decades, and closing the gap may not happen anytime soon.

High Cost of Living

Pay disparities become a greater issue when you factor in the cost of living. The cost of living for a woman is significantly higher than it is for men. Women will pay thousands of dollars more for similar and even the same products or services than men. We tend to spend more on our health plus of course hygiene products put a dent on the finances on a monthly basis.

This extends to insurance policies as well. Women pay more for health insurance plans than men, and because of their specific needs, like becoming pregnant, they will end up paying a great deal more for proper care and essential tests.

Women are having to pay more for essentials while doing so on a paycheck that is far less than a man's pay. These two factors, smaller pay and higher cost of living, are enough to make any woman question their financial literacy. And it's no wonder that women lack the confidence to manage the household on their income alone should anything happen to their husbands.

If single, a woman may struggle to set aside money for emergencies or add to a retirement fund regularly because their pay doesn't allow for it. Many married couples understand the disparities between what a man will be offered and what a woman will be offered. This is why many married couples continue to keep roles of the home divided and which can contribute to why men have more financial say in the marriage. A man is going to get a better deal on a mortgage for the home, car payments, and insurance policy than his wife.

Chapter Highlights

- It was only in the late 1800s that women began to have the same control over their money as men.
- Today, women have greater financial freedom in most countries, but they are still struggling to be viewed as equal to men.
- Women still struggle to maintain financial independence because of societal roles.
- Despite the progress, women are still at a disadvantage when it comes to money matters. Their cost of living is greater, and their paychecks are smaller.

Chapter 2

Financial Independence for Women

"Financial independence is paramount. My Mom always says that when a woman is financially independent she has the ability to love life on her own terms." – Priyanka Chopra

Although women have come a long way in their ability to achieve financial independence, this is not the case around the world. And it hasn't happened without struggle. Women still face issues with receiving inadequate pay and bearing a majority of the responsibility to be the caregiver for children or sick family members. Almost 60 percent of women admit to feeling financially insecure (Lewis-Parks, 2019).

Believe it or not, it wasn't until 1974 when the Equal Credit Opportunity Act was passed that women in the United States were federally ensured a chance to apply for their own line of credit regardless of marital status. This means women were finally legally entitled to be considered for credit cards and home and car loans.

Even though there have been huge strides in equality, women still need to take into consideration their financial well-being. Creating financial independence is not a reflection of your relationship or marriage. Whether you are in a solid relationship or in one that is not going so well, financial independence gives you security for the present and the future. Please don't think you can put off working on financial independence just because money isn't a problem right now.

Why We Need Financial Independence

Circumstances can arise where your entire world gets turned upside down. Suddenly you're responsible for managing the finances of the home while also having to take care of all the other responsibilities you had previously. While you may not want to think that things like divorce can occur, there's no guarantee it will never happen.

Even if you're in the most secure and supportive relationship, sudden illnesses, unexpected death, or the loss of your partner's job can cause financial turmoil. Instead of thinking these things can never happen to you, it's better to plan and feel more secure about your money management.

Divorce

Divorce can happen to any marriage, and if your partner is the primary earner, this can leave you in an even more difficult situation. When divorce happens early in your life, although no less devastating, you can learn to become financially independent and recover. After years of marriage, if you split from your partner, it may be harder to recover and plan for a future.

Unexpected Health Issues or Death

Death is inevitable but most of us tend not to think about it and certainly don't expect it to happen while we're young. But life can throw curveballs and, if you're in the position of losing your partner unexpectedly, you may find yourself under immense financial pressure. Even a major illness can create serious financial burdens that you are not capable of managing simply because you were never a part of paying the household bills or distributing the money.

Also keep in mind that women tend to outlive their male partners by about seven years (Lewis-Parks, 2019). As a woman, you should be educating yourself about insurance policies, retirement funds, and other savings that will keep you financially stable. Also, if you have children, having accounts established for them, whether for college or a trust fund, will give you greater peace of mind if anything were to happen to you and/or your partner.

Financial Stress

Money issues are one of the top five factors that lead to divorce. Paying bills, managing household budgets, and caring for children are all financial stressors that can damage a relationship beyond repair. Wanting and obtaining financial independence will not only eliminate some of the stress from your partner feeling like they have the burden to pay all the bills, but it provides you with the confidence that you aren't always "spending someone else's money".

Women may not be aware of their spending habits in a marriage because they don't sit down and review the bills or income with their partners. They are also not given the opportunity to learn how to save, especially if their partner takes care of paying the bills of the house. While they may do much of the household shopping and ensure their children have what they need, women need to be aware of how much they should be spending or whether they need to cut back if there is no household budget in place.

Most couples fail to discuss their financial lives with one another, and the two just naturally fall into roles of one being the bread winner and the other bearing the household responsibilities. Before you move in with someone or get married to them, there should be a conversation about your combined and separate finances. You should discuss financial goals, plan out debt repayment, and agree on a monthly budget. Unfortunately, most of these matters are rarely discussed or are not discussed as thoroughly as they should be.

Financial stress can cause other issues in the relationship to arise, like infidelity, substance abuse, and poor communication. Keep in mind that wanting to gain financial independence can cause turmoil as well, but this should not deter you from wanting or reaching for financial independence.

Job Insecurity

Job security is not a guarantee. If you are primarily dependent on your partner for income, this can be risky. What happens if the company your partner works for gets sold? What if the company decides to downsize or file for bankruptcy? Thousands of people lose their jobs without notice, and it's something that can happen to anyone. More and more companies are beginning to cut back working hours or eliminate certain job titles altogether as many positions are becoming automated or taken over by computer systems.

When job loss does occur, there is extra stress on your partner to find a job quickly. Many individuals are forced into positions that have fewer benefits and a much smaller pay than they were used to. This can put strain on your relationship.

This is where it can be helpful for you to have an income as well, even if it's small or just a side hustle. A second income will alleviate some of the pressure if the primary breadwinner is laid off. Relying on one income stream is no way to prepare for the future or find security in the present.

What Financial Independence Means

Just because you're married doesn't mean you can't be financially independent. You can still have an active role in your family and home financial plans even if you don't contribute in the form of money. Many things, as noted above, can suddenly occur that will put the burden of managing the household accounts on your shoulders. If you have no say or no knowledge of how money is being spent, you will struggle when trying to manage the unexpected.

Financial independence refers to one's ability to support themselves without the assistance of others or relying on credit cards and loans. For many women, marriage and relationships take away some of this independence because they let their partners handle many of the financial decisions. While there is nothing wrong with this, it's in your better interests to at least be knowledgeable of where the household income is going. You should also have an active say in how this money is being spent.

You should be able to manage your own financial accounts. This means you can create and stick with a budget that allows you to live a comfortable life. You should also know how to stay out of debt, and if you are in debt, you should be able to create an effective debt-repayment plan. You should also be comfortable with making choices about long-term investments, having a savings account, and setting financial goals. Even if you are fine with your spouse or partner managing the finances of the home, at some point, you will inevitably be responsible for the finances. It's much better to be prepared for when this occurs than to feel hopeless, lost, and frustrated when it does.

Remember, you are a couple if you are married, and the rules of the marriage should not be determined by one partner only. If you have kids and you and your partner have agreed that you will stay home to raise the children, this should be something you both have agreed on. It does not mean that they get to make all the decisions that involve the finances of the home just because they are working. Unfortunately, this is what many couples find themselves fighting about.

Domestic Violence

Being in an abusive relationship, physically, emotionally, or mentally, is devastating to put it mildly. Relationships like these pose many barriers and it can feel impossible to escape or be free from the abuse. You have a basic human need and right to feel safe and secure, which is anything but how you feel in a relationship where you are a victim.

This is a sensitive topic. But situations like these can happen to anyone and you must never feel any shame if it happens to you. We all go into relationships expecting and hoping for the best. In the initial heady stages of a relationships it's all too easy to miss danger signs. Some people are also highly skilled at hiding inappropriate personality traits so that even the most savvy woman is fooled.

I can talk about this from personal experience. In my early 20s I was living with a boyfriend who turned violent one night after drinking too much. There had been no obvious signs of this streak before but, looking back afterwards, I had to admit to myself there was a side to him I had chosen to ignore.

Domestic violence may not come in the form of physical abuse. Many women find themselves in abusive situations where they are belittled and made to feel worthless. Money can used as a manipulation tool to keep them in a relationship they would be much better off out of.

If you're experiencing domestic abuse, it's not uncommon that you are also experiencing financial abuse. A partner who controls all of the income and keeps their wallet and accounts on a tight leash can turn into an ugly situation. One of the first red flags of a potentially abusive relationship is when the other person tries to take control of many details of your everyday life. This can include controlling all your financial accounts and forbidding you to work. It leaves you completely helpless and 100 percent dependent on them.

If your partner is unwilling to share account information or sit down and plan out a budget, this can be a sign that things are not right. If your partner doesn't allow you to have access to funds, then you need to establish an income and a way to have access to money when you need it.

Many women in these situations fear for their well-being and their children's safety because they don't have the resources to break away. They often have no support and don't know where they can turn to for the funds to leave.

When It's Time To Go

I'm not going to pretend it's easy to break away from a toxic and abusive relationship. As well as the fear of retribution, we may feel that we have to stay in the marriage so our children still have a father. Or, quite often, we may still love our abuser and live in hope that they will change.

Sorry to be blunt but this is highly unlikely. Unless your partner realizes what they are doing is wrong and can admit it, they are unlikely to get help or be able to change in any meaningful way for any length of time. After I was beaten up by my boyfriend, I moved out then decided I would go back and try to help him by paying for therapy. Yes I know, I know – what was I thinking? But I told myself I loved him and couldn't imagine a future without him. However, the remorse he felt immediately after the attack soon dissipated and he decided he didn't need any help because it wasn't going to happen again. I knew in my heart that wasn't the case. Once that barrier is crossed it will be crossed again. It took a lot of courage to leave for good and, while the physical pain and scars healed relatively quickly, it took a long time to heal the emotional pain.

Leaving might feel like an impossible thing to do but you need to leave for your own sake and the sake of your children. While I was fortunate to not have children and be young enough to go back to my family for support, many women are not in that position. I want you to know that help, support, and services are available to you if you are in a situation like this. So if you're experiencing abuse or know anyone in this situation, please read on.

Resources For When It's Time To Go

In the US, there are many ways you can discreetly begin to build a getaway fund, and there are various programs that will support you. If you have children, some organizations will help you find temporary shelter until you are back on your own two feet. If you are in this type of situation, or know someone who may be, the following services are available. If you are outside the US, check for similar organizations in your country.

Family or friends

The first place you can go is to family and friends. Many women in abusive environments tend to hide their situation from those closest to them, but these should be the people you can find safety and security in. If you have family and friends close by, reach out to them for help. It's not easy to admit what you and your children have been enduring, but to get the help you need, open up to those that love you and care about your safety. Even if you don't have family or friends living near you, they still may be able to help get you to someplace safe, or make arrangements for you to come to them.

Transitional or temporary housing

These are locations that will help you with short-term living arrangements. Depending on your location, this can be communal shelters, scatter-site shelters, or cluster shelters. These shelters provide a safe place for you and your children and will give you the essentials as you prepare to make your next move. Some places to look to help find temporary housing include:

- DomesticShelters.org
- New Hope for Women
- Help USA (based in New York)
- Women Against Abuse (based in Philadelphia, PA)
- 211

While some of these services are location-based, many will be able to set you up with local programs close to you. They have a hotline number to call and are well equipped to be discreet about preparatory plans to get your and your children safely out of your current situation.

Independent Housing

If you already have a financial plan and are making an income, you can find **assistance with renting or purchasing your own home**. Any of the above programs mentioned will be able to guide you in making arrangements to find a home and keep you and your children safe. If this is an option for you, be sure to research your options in terms of insurance and loans. Even if you are renting, consider renter's insurance that will help protect you against unfortunate events. I mention this because it's not uncommon for women in abusive relationships to have unfortunate encounters with their abusers after they have left. If the abuser happens to find where you are living and does anything to the property, the renter's insurance will cover costs incurred due to vandalism or other damages.

Food

When you leave an abusive situation, money will be a concern, and if you have children, getting them the food they need is one of the biggest worries. **Various programs can ensure you have enough food for you and your children.** Your state will have food assistance programs established such as:

- Temporary Assistance for Needy Families (TANF)
- Special Supplemental Nutrition Program for Women, Infants, and Children (WIC)
- Supplemental Nutrition Assistance Program (SNAP)

Each of these programs has its limitations but can be vital. Also, consider local food banks that can provide you with various foods that will help you and your children get by for a few days.

Additional Resources

There are specific resources you can use to help you with your transition out of an abusive relationship. **To help with job opportunities**, look into the following:

1. Dress for Success
2. Her Voice
3. Workforce Innovation and Opportunity Act (WIOA)
4. CareerOneStop
5. ReacHIRE

You may also want to know about organizations that can help with counseling, community support, or other services that right now you might not be considering but later may find valuable. These include:

- National Center on Domestic and Sexual Violence (NCDSV)
- The Allstate Foundation Moving Ahead Curriculum
- Break the Silence Against Domestic Violence
- National Resource Center on Domestic Violence
- National Network to End Domestic Violence (NNEDV)
- Joyful Heart Foundation
- National Endowment for Financial Education (NEFE)
- Steps to End Domestic Violence
- Savvy Ladies

Keep in mind that many unmarried women who find themselves in this situation fear they will have more struggles getting away from their abuser. Even if you are not married, you can use these same services to find help and start over. You can also seek out legal advice to understand what steps you can take to ensure the safety of yourself and your children.

How To Prepare Your 'Escape'

Breaking away from a toxic relationship will require some planning and preparation. Having a plan in place will make it easier to leave when you have the opportunity. Aside from finding the right support, whether it's through friends and family or a program, you need to ensure you have all your important paperwork copied and in a safe space. You can copy things like birth certificates, social security cards, and medical records at your place of work, or you can go to a local stationery store to make copies.

You want to keep the copies in a safe space to have on you when you leave and keep the original copies in another secret location, such as mailing them to a family member. Keeping copies in the cloud is a good idea so long as only you have access to them.

You should try to make copies of all your financial records. If you have a joint account, or if your partner is the primary account holder, you can try to obtain the most recent account information. If the bank is local, you may consider going there personally to see what options you might have to gain access to the funds. Some banks have a dedicated team that assists women in domestic violence situations and can help you set up a secure account with your name on it.

As you are planning for your departure from the relationship, be mindful of how you are contacting others. If you are in a controlling relationship, it's likely that they have access to your phone records and can read text messages. If possible, obtain a temporary phone that your partner will not know you have. You also want to set up a new email address that they won't know about. Always clear your search history if you are using a joint device in your home, and never, never autosave any passwords.

It takes courage to leave an unhealthy relationship, and it can be terrifying. Remind yourself that although this is your situation now, it isn't how you have to live the rest of your life. It is not how your children need to live their lives. You do have the courage to start a new life, and you can regain your independence. Know that there is help available. And once again, please know that this is NOT your fault. I cannot stress enough the importance of not blaming yourself or feeling guilty. There is NOTHING to be ashamed of.

Chapter Highlights

- Even in a happy marriage, you should have a clear understanding of the household finances.
- Divorce is not the only event that can leave you in financial turmoil. Sudden illness or loss of a job can wreak havoc on your happy marriage.
- Planning and preparing for the future with your partner will allow you both to feel financially secure.
- If you are in an abusive situation, know that there is hope and help for you. Even if it's not easy to get yourself out, you do not have to feel trapped in a situation where you are a prisoner.
- If you're in an abusive situation you must NEVER feel guilty or ashamed. This is about your abuser not you.
- Financial independence is not just about having your own money. It's about being able to manage that money and other assets on your own in case anything were to happen.

Chapter 3

Separate Bank Accounts

"Money may not buy love, but fighting about it will bankrupt your relationship." – Michelle Singletary

Creating a separate bank account for yourself provides you with a safeguard in case of an emergency. If something happens to one party, the bank may freeze the joint account. With your own separate account, if anything unfortunate were to happen, you can feel more secure in knowing that you have access to funds in your own account.

Couples plan out their finances and budget in various ways, and there's no right or wrong way to approach this. If you and your partner have a joint account or use a primary account to manage the household expenses, you don't necessarily need to change this if it works for you. However, maintaining a separate account in the event that something unfortunate were to happen provides you with funds to help you get through these events.

For many, having this discussion with their partner is not an easy conversation. You may feel guilty about bringing it up with your partner because they have been the primary provider. You may feel it can cause issues in your relationship and make them feel insecure about your reasons for having a separate account. Everyone is going to react differently when the topic is brought up. You and your partner need to understand that having your own account and being financially independent doesn't mean that there is anything wrong with your relationship. It's about being prepared for the future and ensuring that you and your children will not struggle with finances if something were to happen.

If you and your partner begin working together now to manage the household finances as a team, having your own funds will make more sense. Working together and agreeing on a budget and spending plan for the home will allow each of you to voice your concerns and be heard. In this chapter, you will learn how to have financial conversations with your partner and how to begin to take the first steps in acquiring your own financial independence.

Managing Household Income

When people get married, income gets combined in three common ways: the proportional method, the raw contribution method, and the complete combine method. It's easier to have a joint account to pay for the essentials of the home, but you and your spouse should decide on a method that makes sense for both of you. This should be an agreed-upon choice, and there should be a conversation about how to properly budget this money so you're both working toward achieving the financial goals that matter most to you as a couple and as individuals.

The Proportional Method

With this approach, both individuals contribute to an account and assist in paying the monthly bills contingent on what their income is. The person who makes more money would contribute more than the person earning less money. This approach makes sense and requires both individuals to contribute what they can without feeling like they need to contribute more to keep up with their partner. However, the downside of this method is that the individual who contributes more may feel resentful because they have to pay more because they make more.

The individual contributing less may feel they have less say in the household budget because they contribute less, and the other person contributing more may use this as leverage to make more of the financial choices.

The Raw Contribution Method

Combining accounts with the raw contribution method means each person contributes the same amount, despite their income. This approach can work for some couples as it requires each person to take on half of the financial responsibilities for the household. However, for some couples, this is like having a roommate who needs to pay half of the rent instead of a partner with whom you are building a life. This method can lead to a significant imbalance in the money the lower-income earner has left over to put toward their own financial goals. The individual who earns more will enjoy more financial freedom and less stress.

The Complete Combine Method

The complete combine method is when all accounts are jointly held and accessible by both parties. The couple deposits their income into the same bank account, they have joint credit and debit accounts, retirement funds are shared, and each uses these accounts to pay the bills and make their own personal purchases. This method allows the couple to operate as a team. There is no debate about how much money each person needs to contribute to the household as all money is combined. When all income is combined and a single account is used to pay for the bills, it's much easier to keep track of where the money is going. This method is ideal for couples who have similar spending habits and are clear about their financial goals and future plans. This method can be a disadvantage, though, if one party tends to spend more than the other. If the higher-income earner spends less than the person making less, there can be some frustration over the other person spending money that technically is not theirs to spend.

While each of these methods can work for many couples, they do not take into consideration what happens when one person isn't earning an income. If someone were to lose their job or you are planning on having children, what happens when there is no income coming in from one of you? This is why it's so important to have financial talks with your partner before these instances arise. If you both agree that you will stay home to take care of the kids while your spouse works, what money will you have access to since you will not be contributing?

Talk With Your Spouse

Money is not an easy topic to discuss with your spouse, and there are many ways this can turn into a heated argument. It's important that you and your spouse are on the same page when it comes to the household budget and your own personal financial goals.

Some couples make a choice to combine all their accounts, from their bank accounts to credit cards and retirement funds. Others have a shared account for the household budget and bills while keeping separate accounts for specific savings and personal wants. While it's easier to work from a single account to pay for bills and daily expenses, I still highly recommended that you have a personal account of your own.

Bringing up this topic with your partner is not going to feel comfortable, but the two of you should be sitting down weekly or at least once a month to review your budget and discuss financial goals. Couples who talk about spending and earnings and create a budget together are more likely to stay married. Neglecting this topic can lead to disagreements in the relationship and constant arguments.

While you want to have a serious conversation about the household bills, savings, and other expenses, there are ways you can make this more enjoyable for the both of you.

Have a Financial Planning Date Night

No, it doesn't sound like a romantic candle-lit dinner, but scheduling a date night where you can go over the budget and other financial concerns is something you both need to give your full attention to. You don't want to try to discuss car payments and retirement funds during the weekly football game or while trying to calm your crying baby and coaxing them back to sleep. You both need to agree on a day and time where there will be no distractions. This can be an early breakfast date where you go to your local coffee shop or in the evening after you both cook a meal together and the kids are with your parents.

Part of the budget needs to include a way for you to have access to money in case anything were to happen. This does not have to mean you are planning for divorce, but if your partner were to become ill or be seriously injured, you need to have a way to pay for the bills if they aren't able to.

Create a Budget Together

It doesn't matter who is making more and who is spending more. What matters is that you both come to an agreement together for your current and future life. Creating a budget together is vital, and addressing how money is to be spent should be phrased using 'we' instead of 'you' or 'I.'

Discuss Your Money Mindset and Habits

To be on the same page with the household income and money flow, you both need to address what motivates your spending and saving. By understanding and revealing your outlook on money, you both have a deeper insight as to how you can work together to reach your financial goals.

On one of your first financial planning dates, you should focus on how you were brought up to handle money. It's not easy for anyone to admit they are financially insecure, but this is often rooted in how your family dealt with finances. If you or your partner grew up in a home where one parent handled the money and they never properly taught you how to handle your own money, you're more likely struggle with budgeting and other money matters.

If you or your partner grew up in a home where the household budget was discussed openly, you're more likely to have a better understanding of how to save and spend more wisely.

This first financial date is a time to ask questions of one another. Discuss how each of you feels about your own spending habits and how the finances will be handled. Be clear about what financial independence means for each of you and what each of you is willing to do to achieve it. For example, for you, financial independence might mean contributing more to the household income as well as having a safety net set aside in case anything were to happen to your partner. Or financial independence might simply mean gaining an understanding of the bills and financial obligations that you both should be knowledgeable about.

You may be fine with your partner handling the finances, but you want to know what needs to be paid, when it needs to be paid, and how much needs to go toward those bills.

Along with going over your past and present spending habits, ask each other why you feel you fall on the side of a saver or spender. This will lead you to understand what motivates your spending or saving habits. Find a way you can keep each other on track so that neither of you feels you are doing more than the other. If you tend to err on the side of savings and your partner is more of a spender, find ways to save together and spend on things you both find value in.

During one of your first financial dates, you will want to map out your retirement plans. What does retirement look like for each of you? Is it being able to step away from the workforce completely? Traveling? Spending more time with family? Or, is early retirement something you have your mind set on so you can pursue other passions? It's important to list out your desires for the future so you can both contribute to a plan that will allow each of you to achieve these dreams.

Finally, you also want to address where your finances stand currently. How much debt does each of you have? How much savings do you have? What are your future goals? Are there kids in the present or future? How will you begin saving for them? Most importantly, you need to discuss what happens if there is only one or no income. Each of you may need to make some compromises and sacrifices to achieve your financial goals, but you are in a partnership, and communicating what you are willing to do to become financially independent and successful will lead you to the right path.

Throughout this process, it's important that you both are willing to listen to each other. If one of you is not comfortable with how the budget looks or the contribution method you're using, you need to know why there is uneasiness around this. Maybe one of you feels like an area of your budget needs to be cut back on so you can use that money more wisely, or maybe you want to jumpstart your debt repayment by cutting back on nonessential spending for a few months. Listen to why the other feels something should be changed, and then talk through a solution where you both are comfortable.

Mistakes Will Happen

Pointing fingers or blaming one another for overspending or excess debt is never a good idea. Instead of being upset at yourself or your partner for mishaps in the budget, find out why it happened. Sudden expenses may come up, and when one of you goes over budget because of it, it's best to work out a solution to prevent it from happening again, as opposed to judging one another. Arguing about what is not working with the budget is not going to correct the problem—making adjustments will.

Chapter Highlights

- Set a date to talk with your spouse/partner to go over financial concerns.
- Discuss what contribution method you both are comfortable with to cover household expenses.
- Be clear about why it's important for you and your partner to keep separate accounts to ensure you are prepared for the future.
- Create a budget with your partner and understand what expenses need to be paid.

- Make it a weekly, or at the very least, monthly priority to sit down and go over your budget.
- Be open about your spending habits and issues that you struggle with, whether this is spending too much or being too anxious over savings.

Chapter 4

Track Your Spending

"The shortest period of time lies between the minute you put some money away for a rainy day and the unexpected arrival of rain." – Jane Bryant Quinn

Financial independence is not just about having your own account or having little debt. Knowing what you are spending on and identifying spending habits, both good and bad, will lead to better money management skills. It's important that you know what assets you have, whether these are joint or individually. The first real step to financial independence is tracking what you spend and creating a list of your assets. This will guide you to creating better spending habits and allow you to create and stick with a realistic budget.

Knowing your basic expenses is not enough to gain control over your money. You may know that you spend $400 on rent, $50 on utilities, $50 on medical expenses, and $100 on your cell phone. You have in your mind that your expenses add up to $600 a month, and you estimate that you spend around $100 on other nonessentials each week. After you track your spending for a week, you realize you are spending around $60 a week on nonessentials, which you think is great! When you take a closer look at where that $60 went, you realize that half of it is being spent on your two-coffee-a-day-habit from the gourmet coffee shop around the corner from where you work.

Things like coffee may not feel like an expense as you can easily make it yourself or get it for free from the break room, so you fail to consider how much each one of those delicious special brews is costing you. With this knowledge, you can choose whether you need to cut back or eliminate this expense to put your money to better use.

Some of you will feel like you have a great handle on your spending, and tracking this will either prove this to be correct or shine a light on where you need to be more mindful about your spending habits. The data you gather from your tracking experience is also great to bring up with your partner during your weekly financial dates. You can suggest that they track their spending as well. As you will learn in this chapter, there is a lot you can learn about your views on money and spending.

List Your Assets and Liabilities

First, it's a good idea to to work out your current financial position. If you are married, you and your spouse should have a variety of assets together, but each of you most likely has individual assets as well. Personal assets are items that have a monetary value. If you and your partner own a home, your home is an asset. Your bank accounts, retirement funds, stocks, or other investments are also assets.

It's important that you understand what assets you have individually and together with your partner and assess their value. Assets can increase or decrease in value over time. Are your assets generating more cash flow, or will they deplete in value?

For any assets obtained through marriage, you want to know whose name is listed as the primary holder. For example, when you got married, you may have moved into your spouse's home, and the house was probably already in their name. If anything were to happen to your spouse, you need to know what will happen to the home and how you will be able to maintain it.

Depending on your location, it can be difficult to get utilities transferred into your name if your name was never added to the homeownership papers. Little things like this are often never thought of, but they can cause a great deal of stress and add additional cost to get the utilities transferred into your name.

Along with assets, you also need to be aware of your liabilities, individually and jointly. Liabilities are your debts, which include credit card debt, student loans, mortgages, and unpaid taxes. You are also responsible for loans that you have cosigned for, so these should be included in your list of liabilities. Liabilities are essential for creating a household budget because, for many people, a majority of their income is spent on paying off these debts.

Trying to hide a substantial amount of debt or remaining in the dark about how much debt you and your partner have will cause serious issues with your budgeting. This is especially true if you plan to buy a new home or apply for any type of loan. When you're married, it's not uncommon for lenders to look at the credit of both you and your partner. If one or both of you have a high number of liability accounts, this can hinder you from being approved for the loan.

It's important for both of you to know which debts need to be paid, how much is going to be dedicated to paying them off, when they need to be paid each month, and when you expect to have each balance eliminated. Along with these debts, you both also need to be aware of the common household bills that need to be paid; jointly look over things like the cable, electricity, and heating bills as well as property taxes. Many utility bills can be reduced and provide you with a significant amount of extra money that can be put to better use either for debt repayment or savings.

You can download a free Budget Planner Bundle, which includes a printable template to help with putting this list together, at www.zoemadden.com.

Tracking Your Spending

Next you need to work out where all your money is going. Falling into the thought process of "It only costs a dollar," is easy. Then you don't worry about tracking that dollar, but those dollars add up. Tracking your spending does take a conscious effort, and many people find that when they track, they will often spend less. Be aware that you are spending less because you are tracking where your money is going.

While spending less is a good thing, you also need to be conscious of spending habits when you're not keeping a close eye on where your money is going.

You need to watch those direct debits so make a list of all your subscriptions and monthly bills. You can use this information when you set up your monthly budgets. Another benefit of tracking subscriptions in this way is you may see some you don't really need that can be cancelled.

Check Your Accounts

Know where you are starting from. Before you begin tracking, review all of your accounts. How much do you have in your bank account, what are the balances on your credit cards, and do you keep cash on hand? Also, know how much income you have coming in. Whether you have an income or your partner is the primary income generator, you want to know how much you have to work with.

Organize Your Expenses

This is where many people become discouraged. They see everything that needs to get paid and realize they have very little to spend on other things they want or need. This does not have to be the case. While your expenses might feel overwhelming, remember that you are going to track what you actually spend so that you know what you have to work with.

Expenses refer to anything that your money is going toward. It's important to differentiate between essential and nonessential expenses. Essential expenses are those you need to pay for your survival and overall well-being, such as your rent or mortgage, food, medication, and savings. Nonessentials are the things that you spend on that you can live without, such as going out for coffee, going out to the movies, or buying another pair of shoes when you already own five pairs. Ahem, I included that last one as I've been a little guilty of doing such things in the past. While a majority of your expenses can be easily categorized as essential or nonessential, you want to further break down these lists.

Essentials may be monthly, quarterly, or yearly. Your quarterly and yearly expenses will be broken down into small manageable monthly payments that you will put aside until you know they are due. For example, you know that in June each year, you will have to come up with $400 to cover your car insurance. Instead of waiting until May or June to figure out how to account for this $400, you will set aside money every month so you have the money when it comes time to pay. You will also have fixed and variable expenses. Fixed expenses will remain the same each month. Variable expenses can be flexible and adjusted on a month-to-month basis, such as your food or gas for the car.

Nonessentials should be listed in a way that will allow you to see what you can either reduce or cut from your budget to make better use of your money. You may love your Saturday brunches but spending $50 every week may be better allocated to a savings account. Instead of going out for brunch, you can stay in and make your own. Or, you may have a love for seeking out custom-made jewelry pieces on Etsy. Although you know you can do without this expense, it's something that makes you feel good, not just for the jewelry but because you are supporting other independent women. This may be something you can, however, feel comfortable about cutting back on. And yes I've been guilty again here.

Use a Template or App to Help You Track

Once you have a general idea about what you need and think you spend money on, it's time to start tracking where the money is actually going. You want to track for up to four weeks. This may seem like a lot but for the first week, you will certainly be more conscious of your spending, and this will give you a false idea of what your spending is truly like. When tracking, you want to track every penny you spend. If you gave your niece $10 for her birthday, track it. If you spend an extra $2 at the checkout for a candy bar, it gets tracked.

You can use an app on your phone to take notes on what you are spending. Some bank accounts will allow you to set up a budget so you can automatically see when money is getting withdrawn from your account and where it is going. You may even be able to set up a maximum spending limit which will allow you to identify where you are over or underspending.

Some easy to use apps for tracking your money flow include:

- Mint
- You Need a Budget (YNAB)
- PocketGuard
- EveryDollar
- Goodbudget
- Honeydue
- Fudget
- Daily Budget Original
- Zeta
- Simplifi
- Clarity Money

Many of these apps will connect to your current banking and credit accounts, and some will allow you to manually add items that you spend money on. The Honeydue app lets you track your joint spending if you are married or in a relationship. Use one that fits your needs and that you will actually use. Just downloading the app isn't going to get you anywhere!

You can also create a spreadsheet that will help you fill in what you have spent at the end of the day. Don't leave anything out. You can create a spreadsheet yourself using software like Microsoft Excel, or you can download your free Budget Planner Bundle at www.zoemadden.com. The bundle includes a Subscriptions Tracker, a Monthly Bills Tracker and a Spending Tracker.

Some things are minimally priced, so you will not feel like you should be concerned about how much you spend on them, but when you add these up, it can equal hundreds of dollars you could spend in a more proactive manner.

Review Weekly

Reviewing your tracker on a weekly basis will help you see what you can cut immediately or what you may want to cut in the future. This is the only way you will honestly learn how much you are spending and saving. At the end of each week, take time to review your account balances and look at receipts for any purchase you made with cash.

From this weekly review, some habits may jump out at you as a surprise, such as the $100 you spend for lunch every week, even though you only buy a salad and drink. You will also be surprised by where you are not spending as much as you thought you were. For example, you may think that your unusual need to buy office supplies would easily take $50 out of your pocket each week, but it has only accounted for $10 of your weekly expenses.

There will be things to address, but you do not want to berate yourself or feel discouraged after you review your weekly spending. We're doing this to build awareness around your money, not to discourage you. Tracking will help you build more confidence and help you take better control of your finances. Without tracking, you may never acknowledge your $20 a day salad overspending habit, and you might have continued to spend this amount for much longer. Once you know better, you can do better.

Your Spending Habits

There are good and not-so-good spending habits, and these have to do with how you spend your money as well as your thought process around financial matters. As mentioned before, many people who do not spend wisely often do so because they were never properly taught how to manage their money. Parents often neglect to teach their children how to manage money and most of us freely spend our pocket money safe in the knowledge that more will be given to us next week.

Schools rarely include money management in the curriculum. They spend a lot of time teaching us how to work for money then let us loose into the world completely ignorant of how to make money work for us.

Worse still, young adults are never taught about debt or how to avoid it. Banks are sneaky and offer "get it for free now" options if young people sign up for accounts or credit cards well before they have any sense of what they are getting themselves into.

Even if we don't yet have enough proper financial knowledge, we're not going to use this as an excuse to continue with unhelpful spending habits. Instead, we'll look at addressing, correcting, and replacing them with financially freeing habits.

Too Many Nonessentials

Up until you began to track where your money was going, you may have been completely unaware of how many nonessential purchases you make every day.

From buying lunch during the workweek to spontaneous online deals you can't ignore, these nonessential and often impulse buys average out to be $50 a day (Egan, 2020). We don't feel guilty about making these purchases because they are so insignificant at the moment, but when you begin to realize that everything adds up, you are spending close to, if not more than $18,000 for nonessential items that are not adding much value to your life. This is money that could be spent much more wisely.

You don't have to eliminate all nonessential items from your budget. In fact it's a good idea to keep a few things. Nonessentials should, however, be things that you value and enjoy the most or those that cannot be replaced by a more cost-efficient solution, like filling up a large water bottle at home to take with you to work instead of buying a few bottles during your workday.

There are a few ways to address this bad habit of overspending on nonessentials:

- **Leave your credit and debit cards at home.** From a psychological standpoint, using physical money to pay for purchases makes you stop and question whether you really need everything you are buying. This is also a good way to combat impulse purchases. If you can only spend the cash you have on hand, you'll think twice about buying anything you didn't initially intend on purchasing when you got to the store.

- **Evaluate how much you spend on food in total, not just on groceries**. While groceries are essential, food purchases can make up a majority of nonessential spending. Eating out, stopping at the drive-thru, purchasing your lunch instead of packing it, and stopping to grab a quick snack or coffee adds up to hundreds of dollars a month that could be saved. Cooking at home and prepping your breakfast, lunch, and snacks for the week can help you save more and allow you to put your money where it is needed. Along with saving you money, home-cooked meals are often healthier than fast foods. While you can certainly treat yourself to a nice meal out every once in a while, reconsider if what you are spending on food for the month is the best use of your money.

- **Ask yourself if you are purchasing a need or a want.** We try to justify some of our nonessential purchases as a need when they are a want. You may think you need to get a new pair of shoes, but this is more likely a want. Even on bigger purchases, like upgrading your mobile phone or buying a new TV, you may feel you are in need of something new but are these wants?
  These examples may appear to be obvious wants, but how many times have you honestly made a purchase because you convinced yourself it was something you needed to have when truly it was just a want? If you do find yourself in a situation where you are contemplating a wanted item, pause and consider what this purchase is really costing you. Even if you can afford it, would the money spent on this item be of better use going somewhere else, like a savings account or to debt repayment?
  Before you make a nonessential purchase, give yourself at least one day to reconsider spending the money. If, after a day, you still have a great desire for this item, and you have considered that the money spent on this item will not set you back in other areas of your budget, then by all means, go get yourself that new pair of shoes.

- **Avoid sale traps**. I know from personal experience how hard it is to resist a great deal and discount, but making a purchase just because you got a good deal on it isn't the best way to spend your money. Unless the item on sale is something you really need, avoid looking for a great sale to justify making unnecessary purchases.

- **Do you know what subscriptions you have?** Many people have hundreds of dollars going toward subscriptions they have never used and will never use. Monthly subscriptions seem like a great idea at the time you sign up for them, but after a few months, they are often unused and even forgotten about. Millions of people sign up for a gym membership at the beginning of each year. They go for a few weeks and then stop going. For months, they convince themselves they are going to start going back to the gym because they are paying for the monthly membership but never do. This is just a waste of money.

Magazine subscriptions, cable television, apps you never open, and video streaming services can be added to your nonessential cash flow. Review your subscription fees and see where you can make some cuts, and do so honestly. If you haven't used it in two or more months, are you going to get your money's worth out of it? Eliminating a few subscription fees can free up thousands of dollars a year that you can use for other essentials.

Cut Up Those Credit Cards

There are many reasons why you want to cut back and, if possible, eliminate using credit cards for your purchases. It can be easy to rack up thousands of dollars in credit card debt, and even worse, these cards often have high-interest rates that will keep you stuck with thousands more in debt.

Using credit cards gives you a false sense of having more money than you actually have to spend. Any amount of credit card debt will hinder your financial goals because those interest charges waste your money.

Even if you never miss a payment, most of the payments you make may only cover the interest that is accumulated. If you do miss a payment, this can quickly turn into two or three missed payments. Your credit score will plummet, it will be difficult to take out a loan, you may not be hired for some jobs, and you can be rejected from rental properties. A high amount of credit card debt can lead to bankruptcy, setting you back years as you try to repair your credit and build up your wealth.

If you do have a tendency to rely on your credit cards, there are ways to combat this bad habit. While debt repayment will be covered in more detail later in this book, know that it can be accomplished.

First, if you have outstanding balances on your credit cards, make more than the monthly payments to bring the balance to zero. Next, if you are going to use your credit card, treat it like your bank card. Do not charge what you can't afford to pay off immediately. Third, stick to a budget and put a limit on how much or what you can use the credit card for. Fourth, leave your credit cards at home. It will be easy to reach for your card and use it out of habit if you have it on you or near you.

You can completely avoid the temptation and accidental use by not having credit cards on you. Finally, go through all your favorite online stores and remove your stored credit card information. Having the option to "Buy Now" without entering your card information makes overspending easier. By removing your card information, you will significantly reduce your online impulse spending.

Another good reason to cancel your credit cards is that credit card limits are also taken into account when you apply for loans from banks. While it might be nice to think you have a $15,000 limit "in case you need it", that $15,000 will be counted as a loan when your serviceability is assessed. It could mean the difference between being granted the loan or being turned down. It's much better to have an amount set aside in an emergency savings account that you only dip into if something truly urgent comes up.

Having Long-Term Savings

Purchasing a home or setting aside for your children's college fund or retirement are all long-term financial goals that many never set money aside for. These huge expenses require years of saving, but many people are not preparing for them as early as they can. Unless you begin to think about your long-term desires and start taking action now, you may never afford that home, and retirement may be delayed by years.

If you are over the age of 25 and have yet to start a future savings account, it's not too late to start, but the older you get, the harder it will be to achieve the desired savings that you set out to create.

Luckily, starting a fund for your future accounts is easy to do. If you set up a high-yield savings account and have money automatically deposited into it each month, you can begin to build up small savings. Chances are you will never miss this money and it will slowly build up. And by taking the initiative to cut back your spending, you can transfer any extra money to this account.

Shop Around

Just because you've always used one electricity or cable provider doesn't mean you need to stay with them. Compare plans. If you find a better deal, ask the company you're currently with if they can match the price. If they can't then switch. Similarly, always get more than one quote when it comes to renewing insurances and go for the one that's best (make sure you compare like for like and don't lose any benefits you may need). You could save hundreds of dollars a year by doing this.

Be Serious With Your Budget

A budget gives you complete control of your finances, but if you don't use it, it defeats the whole purpose. Creating a budget allows you to map out exactly how you can accomplish your short and long-term financial goals. Neglecting to stick to your budget and overspending or skipping on paying what you intend to pay on debt is not going to lead you to financial independence.

In the next chapter we'll look at how you can make a budget work for you and the best tips for sticking to a budget.

Chapter Highlights

- Know where you stand now and where you want to go with your money.
- Understand what assets and liabilities you and your partner currently have.
- Track every purchase you make for up to four weeks. Use an app or notebook to record everything you are spending money on.
- Identify poor spending habits and come up with a plan to combat them.
- Start with one thing at a time, as trying to change everything all at once is going to cause you more frustration, and you will only beat yourself up for failure.
- Be honest with yourself about why you are making certain purchases and if or how you can make better choices that will move you forward to financial independence.
- You can download your free Budget Planner Bundle to help you track where your money is going at www.zoemadden.com.

Chapter 5

The Dreaded "B" Word... Budget

"A budget is telling your money where to go instead of wondering where it went." – Dave Ramsey

Budgeting is hard. It's a little like dieting. When we diet, we tell ourselves what we can and cannot eat. We feel guilty if we slip up and eat something we're not allowed, and then we impose even stricter guidelines to follow. Eventually, all the "No, I can't eat that because I am on a diet" catches up, and we binge. Budgeting instills the same fears. We put restrictions on what we can do with our money, and this leaves us feeling deprived. When we become overwhelmed by the deprivation, we splurge, then we feel guilty and try to create even more rules on what we can spend on. It turns into a vicious cycle where we often abandon our budgets and continue with bad spending habits.

It's not the budget that we have a problem with. It's our mindset around having to create a budget that causes us problems. The budget is just a list of things we plan to spend our money on. Our mindset tells us we aren't allowed to spend on other things, and more importantly, that if we do not stick to the budget, then we fail. We need to address our hesitation in creating a budget.

Many of us feel a budget highlights our money issues instead of empowering us to gain control. Instead of focusing on what we are not doing with our money, we should feel proud that we have made the conscious choice about what we will spend it on. When we shift this focus and take responsibility for our spending, we begin to overcome the bad habits like impulse spending that make us feel guilty for not sticking with our financial plans.

First, let's take a look at why most people struggle with creating a budget and how we can map out our finances in a more effective manner.

Why Budgets Don't Usually Work

There's no denying that budgeting can a tedious task. It's all too easy to convince ourselves we have a good enough handle on our finances to not need one. No matter how confident or unsure you are about your money situation, tracking where your money comes from and where it goes is the only way to take control of your finances. Trying to do this math in your head and keep track of your future goals isn't possible without a clear, written plan.

Unfortunately, most people, and we're talking men and women alike, do not know how to properly create a budget. Without the knowledge of what a budget is supposed to provide, things can go wrong and often do. Individuals who have tried to follow a budget quickly abandon it because it doesn't work for them, and there are few good reasons why:

Your budget is unrealistic

While it's commendable that you want to change all your poor spending habits overnight, you need to be honest with yourself. You need to think clearly about what you can and can't spend on certain expenses.

If you're buying groceries for a house of four, allocating just $100 for groceries each month is probably going to set you up for failure unless you have some amazing couponing skills.

While you certainly want to be mindful about spending more than necessary, you also need to be realistic that you'll have to spend more on some things.

No clear 'why' for sticking with a budget

This is something that is easily neglected. We all want to have stellar spending habits where we have enough to pay for the essentials and some left over to enjoy ourselves. Unfortunately, this probably won't motivate you to stick to a budget. You need to set goals and have something to work toward.

This can be something longer term like saving for a new car or family vacation. You can also have short-term goals like being able to buy a nice dress and shoes for an upcoming wedding or splurge a little for your kid's birthday. Having goals not only provides you with motivation but also gives you something to track against to ensure you are staying on the right path.

Others influence your spending habits

You've probably heard the saying "you are who you surround yourself with," meaning your inner circle influences your behaviors and thought processes. If your close friends and family do not take their finances seriously and spend irresponsibly, you're more likely to keep those same spending habits.

You don't have to ditch your friends to improve your finances, but you do need to be aware of how you spend when you're around your friends and which of them impacts your spending. It can be incredibly hard to save and stick with a debt repayment plan when everyone else around you appears to be able to spend whatever they want whenever they want. This can cause you to become jealous because you feel like you are the only one struggling financially. Or it can lead to giving in to temptation because you want to spend as freely as they seem to.

Whether it's a family member or a friend, be aware of those you need to impress with how much you spend. Who do you hang out with that causes you to spend a little or a lot more when you go out? It can be easy to justify a huge bill after a much-deserved night out with the girls, but this is only going to derail your budget.

Most friends will understand you are working toward financial goals, and they will be supportive. They will even find low-key activities to do to help them save too. Don't feel like you can't have a social life on your way to financial independence, but do be aware of what will stand in your way of getting there.

You're not being flexible with your budget

It may take a few months before you reach a point where you are somewhat comfortable with your budget. If after the first month you realize you grossly neglected one area of your spending, this does not mean you throw in the towel.

Creating a budget is a process of trial and error, and it will need adjustments as you go. If you don't take the opportunity to make these adjustments, you're never going to reach your financial goals. Keep in mind that while you may find your calculations in one area have been way off, you may also notice you were able to save significantly more in other areas.

Take the time to review your budget and go into the review with the intention of improving it. You need to allow for things to be changed to get a better fit, but do not give up. I know it can be frustrating. By nature, we want things to work out the right way the very first time, and budgeting takes time and a lot of effort. If you're willing to stick with it and put in the effort, you'll be rewarded in the short and long term.

There's no room for fun spending

A budget doesn't mean you have to cut back on all the leisurely items or any of the fun stuff you enjoy. Instead, a budget allows you to properly factor in these things so you can enjoy them even more. Many people think they need to have a strict budget that only allows them to pay bills and add to their savings, but doing this is going to hurt your goals more than it will progress them. When you create your budget, you need to allocate money to the things you enjoy. This is essential for creating a budget that will work for you. Remember, depriving yourself of these wants is only going to cause you to be resentful and eventually forgo your budget altogether.

Your budget doesn't align with your lifestyle or needs

This happens when you use a pre-made template or follow too closely what others tell you your budget needs to include. While using templates and seeking advice for best practices on how to create an effective budget is a good idea, it can lead to disappointment. Your budget needs to be created around your income and needs, with your future wants, both short and long term, in mind.

Your budget doesn't plan for future expenses

Big financial hits like having to take the car to the mechanic or replacing a hot water tank will derail your spending. These things always seem to come at us out of nowhere, but the truth is they are not as unexpected as they should be. We know that big expenses and emergencies like these will occur—we just fail to plan for them. When they do hit, we're completely thrown off, and it takes months or even longer to recover.

We can lessen the blow of these by setting aside a little each month for such emergencies. While we cannot see the future and know exactly when sudden expenses are going to arise, we do know they will inevitably happen. With this understanding and acceptance, we can better prepare ourselves so that when they suddenly pop up, we are not frantically trying to find the money to pay for them.

You don't address spending issues

The main reason people struggle with budgeting is that they neglect their poor spending habits. If you know you are an impulse shopper and, despite your best effort, you continuously overspend, you need to find a solution for these habits. This might mean you go to the store with only cash and leave the credit cards and bank cards at home so you don't buy what you do not need.

Your budget doesn't account for annual payments or spending

How many times have the holidays come around, and you are stressing about not having the money to buy gifts or do the holiday meal shopping? What about when car insurance or taxes come around? Too many of us scramble to find the money to pay for these annual payments, and this often leads us to have to skimp for months after we make the payment. Like big emergency expenses, these need to be a part of your monthly budget, not just the month they are due. By setting aside a little each month to pay for these once-a-year items, you will feel less stressed and derailed.

It's a Spending Plan, Not a Budget

Instead of thinking of it as a budget, consider it a spending plan—one where you allocate a purpose to every penny you have coming in. Nothing gets set aside without a purpose. This will lead to much wiser spending. When your money has a purpose, you're less inclined to spend impulsively.

A mistake many people make is to go through their spending plan, notice they have $10 left, and then think they can just spend it whenever. What tends to happen is, since that $10 is not allocated to a specific account, you can't track when it has been spent or if there is anything left over to spend. So, you overspend because you had those ten extra dollars at the beginning of the month, but by the end of the month, you spent two or three times more than that.

For us to stick with a budget, we need to reframe how we look at our money; saving it, spending it, and managing it. With a spending plan, we are focused on our financial goals. When we use a spending plan, we are not restricting ourselves. Instead, we are taking into consideration the things we enjoy and want more of. We use this to create a plan that allows us to achieve those things.

Benefits of a Spending Plan

Whether you call it a budget or a spending plan, there are big benefits to sticking

Some key categories that your monthly spending plan may include:

- Housing (rent or mortgage)
- Insurance
- Transportation (car payments, gas, maintenance, saving for a new car)
- Utilities
- Food and household items
- Entertainment
- Clothing and other essentials
- Emergency fund
- Retirement fund
- Future big expenses
- Annual expenses

Keep in mind that your monthly spending plan may have many more categories. If you pay for child care, this will need to be included. If you pay to put your kids in private school, this will need to be broken down and added to monthly spending. You also want a fun money category and other savings categories.

Before you start getting overwhelmed with how many categories you plan, keep in mind that every dollar that comes in will have a purpose. Your goal is to assign every dollar that comes in to an account, so your balance for the month is going to equal zero.

As you are breaking your plan into categories, consider having a separate account for certain payments and savings. For example, you can have an account that is dedicated to your daily expenses or more regular expenses like groceries and gas. Open up a savings account for your emergency fund, and have a monthly deposit set up so you will not have to worry about doing this yourself each month. Then have a cash fund for your splurge items.

The more things you can automate, the easier it will be for you to track your spending and ensure that your money is going where it needs to go. Setting up different savings accounts with a predetermined amount to be deposited every month will keep you on track.

You can download a free Budget Planner Bundle, which includes Spending Plan template, at www.zoemadden.com.

Chapter Highlights

- Give your money a purpose. Every dollar you have coming in should have an account or purpose that it goes toward. No dollar gets left behind.
- Do not treat your budget like a diet. Allow for flexibility and enjoyment.
- Reframe the way you think of a budget. It's not about what you can't do with your money but instead what you can do.
- Determine what type of budgeting system works best for you (envelope method, creating different accounts, using one primary account).
- Review your budget monthly to ensure it fits with your lifestyle and future goals.
- Download your free Budget Planner Bundle at www.zoemadden.com.

Chapter 6

Investing

"How many millionaires do you know who have become wealthy by investing in savings accounts? I rest my case." – Robert G. Allen

It doesn't matter at what age you begin investing—it is never too late to get started. Many people think of investing as a luxury, and those who have high-paying jobs and are already wealthy are the only ones who can invest. This is so far from the truth.

Investing is one of the best things you can do to make your money work for you. It creates a passive income stream that will allow you to save for the future and leave a solid inheritance for your children. Even after retirement, you can begin investing for the sole purpose of providing for your children or grandchildren long after you are gone.

You may have the impression that investing is complex and time-consuming. While some investments do require a thorough understanding of the market and tax impacts, many simply require you to know what your goals are and to understand your options.

Don't think it's possible? Think you are too old? Let me tell you about Bonnie. *Now, Bonnie did have impeccable organizational skills. She had a secure govern-*

ment job working at the post office, and her retirement and pension were enough to allow her to live comfortably after retirement. She retired at the age of 68, and she knew that she wanted to do more for her children after she was gone. She began reading and learning everything she could, reached out to financial advisers and asked questions, and negotiated better deals on her insurance plans so she could put more away for her children. She opened up an investment fund for both her children, but she set it up so her name was the primary holder and her children's names were listed as secondary account holders. When she learned she would become a grandmother, she opened an account for her grandchildren. She added to all the accounts throughout her retirement and took pride in watching their balances grow. When she passed, her children could easily remove her name from the accounts and access the funds without having to go through endless lawyers and pay exuberant fees. She was able to leave them a sizeable inheritance.

Bonnie's story will look different than yours. But the main point to take from it is that it doesn't matter what age you are when you start to invest, but it does matter that you start now. This chapter will provide you with the information to get started. Even if you only have a little to invest now, you can grow that investment over the years.

Please note that, as mentioned earlier in this book, the information here is generally factual and does not take your personal circumstances into account. It isn't financial advice or financial product advice in any way. Do your own research into any of the products mentioned and consider seeking independent financial advice tailored to your needs from a licensed or authorized financial advisor.

Savings Versus Investing

Creating savings for emergencies and planning for big expenses in the future is essential. But, creating savings is also for short-term goals. When you are adding money to a savings account, you are setting it aside little by little. If you want to buy a new house, you put a little money away each month so that in a few years, you have enough for a down payment. Savings accounts are set up to put your money toward a purchase or product.

You should also focus on setting up an emergency fund. Emergency funds have been mentioned a few times throughout this book, but it's an important savings account that most people do not consider making a priority. A three-month emergency fund is the bare minimum you want, and six months to a year is what you want to continue to work toward.

You should continue adding to this fund every month. This emergency fund should cover all your expenses if you are unable to work or there is no income coming into the home.

The right investing can help you create a passive income to achieve your financial goals for the long term. When you invest, you are buying another asset, like a rental property or stocks, in hopes that the value of that product will increase.

Investing can yield big rewards, but the bigger the rewards often means the risk is greater. You invest with the intention of your investment growing over time. Unlike a savings account, an investment is not just putting your money somewhere until you have enough to use it for what you want. Investing is a thought-out process to make your money work more for you.

Why You Should Be Investing

You can do all the research possible, and you may still be uncertain if investing is the right option for you. Any financial expert is going to tell you that investing is one of the best ways to reach short or long-term financial goals. It's the easiest way to make your money continuously work for you. Some of the ways investing can benefit you include:

1. **Bigger returns**
   Legendary investor Warren Buffett has called compound interest an

investor's best friend, since it earns returns not only on your initial investment but on the interest you accumulate too. Over time, these small interest payments add up adding more interest to your initial balance even if you never put more of your money into it. The earlier you start your investment, the more compounding interest will get added and the bigger your savings grows. This is how you make your money work smarter for you and not harder.

2. **Plan for retirement**

   I have mentioned retirement a lot because it's so important that you begin planning for it now rather than later. Millions of people neglect retirement funds, and as they get older, they realize there is no possible way for them to retire at 65 or even 75. They begin to stress and fear retirement because they simply will not have enough to cover their cost of living. Becoming an investor at any age will provide you with the opportunities to retire with less worry and fear.

3. **Achieve financial success**

   With investing, you are making your money work for you. You can keep your money secure in a bank account, but it's just sitting there. Even if you place it in an interest-earning savings account, you may get a low interest rate on your balance. This is hardly making your money work. Through investing, you reach your financial goals by growing your wealth. You have already put in the work and earned your pay. Investing allows you to get the most out of that pay by building on top of it. Additionally, you get to determine what financial success means for you. For many, the investment provides financial success in the form of college funds, retirement security, and vacations. For others, it means they can choose to quit their nine to five jobs to pursue more meaningful careers and work on their own terms. By investing, you get to create your own financial freedom and live life more on your own terms.

If you're employed and have not looked at your company's investment opportunities, do not hesitate to do so now. If your partner isn't taking advantage of the investment opportunities their company offers, it's something you both need to sit down and discuss. Many companies have retirement plans that not only allow you to contribute to a retirement fund through various investments, but many will offer to match your contributions. If your company or your partner's company does not offer investment opportunities, you can still invest on your own. As you will learn, you do not need to understand all the complexities of investing. You do not need to follow any intricate investment strategy—but you do need to start now, even if it's with very little.

Best Investment Strategies

Investments should be a part of your long-term financial goals. Making short-term investments can increase your chances of loss. Look at your five-plus-year goals. How can investing help you achieve those goals? These can include things like retirement, paying for your kids' college fees, and buying a larger home.

Diversification can lead to bigger and better returns on your investments. Spreading your money across a few investment types can minimize your risk as well. Since you're not putting all your money in one place, you're not relying on that one investment to be a huge success.

Pro Investment Tips

Do not procrastinate. Putting off investing will result in financial losses and put you behind on the goals you want to reach. Many people put off investing either because they don't feel they have the extra funds to start investing or because they are afraid of how much they will lose if they make the wrong investments. Both are legitimate concerns but consider where else you spend your money.

Though it may take some adjustment, it can be possible to find an extra hundred dollars to invest. As far as concerns over losses, it's likely that you may make a few unsuccessful investments and lose a little. But, unless you are going big and all in, you are not going to lose everything. Yes, a loss can happen, but as long as you make choices according to your risk tolerance, you will almost always come out on top.

It's easier than ever to learn the fundamentals of investing and take advantage of different investment strategies and avenues to build up a legacy of wealth. Most investing apps or websites offer training and additional resources that will simplify the process.

Many of the top investment professionals are willing to share the best approaches to see the biggest returns on your investment for free. Some even offer a training guide. There are many places you can turn to in order to get ahead and gain the knowledge to make wise and successful investments. You just have to take the initiative to find them.

You do need to be patient though. While some stock investments may reward you with huge returns in a short time frame, most will grow steadily over time. Investments are great long-term strategies for using your money wisely. Do not get caught up in checking how much your investment is growing too often. As long as it's growing, you are on the right path.

Many people become anxious and impatient when they don't see hundreds or thousands added to their accounts over a few months, but as years go by, they see a substantial balance that is well worth the wait. Remain focused on your long-term goals and avoid getting caught up in the slow growth.

Before You Invest

Before you get started with investing, you should be clear about whether you are ready to invest or not. While the idea of investing, once you gain a greater understanding of it, is very appealing, it can lead to serious losses you might not recover from.

It's important that before you invest, you understand that you should NEVER invest money that you are not willing or able to lose. There are some investment strategies that carry a much lower level of risk, so even those who can't afford to lose can still take advantage of some investment avenues. Ask yourself the following before you start investing to be sure it is the right choice for you based on your current financial standing.

1. **Do you have debt?** Having a small amount of debt should not keep you from getting started with investing, but if you have a significant amount of debt, you want to work on getting that paid off first. Credit card debt is the most important debt to get rid of first. Once you have this taken care of and your other debts are easily managed, then you could begin to invest.

2. **What are your short and long-term goals?** Your goals will direct you to the best investment options. Some investments will allow you to reach your short-term goals while still working toward long-term goals. Know what you want to accomplish and when you want to accomplish it. You will have a clear roadmap to follow with more than enough time to accomplish what you set out to do.

3. **How long will your emergency fund last?** An emergency fund gives you financial security. In the event that something were to happen, you want to have an emergency fund to rely on instead of having to pay high fees to withdraw money from an investment fund. Before you invest, you want to have your emergency fund established that will last you at least three months and you should be able to add to it while you are investing.

4. **Do you know what your investment options are?** We will cover a few

of your investment options in the next section, but you want to have a good idea of what your options are. For short-term investment, where you will be using the money in five years or less, you want to put your money in an account that has less risk attached to it. Since you will need this money sooner rather than later, you want to ensure that you have the money to use when you need it.

For more long-term investments, you can look at choosing higher-risk investment options. A higher-risk option will yield better results, but on the off chance that you meet a loss, you have time to recover from it.

Best Beginner Investments

You may have avoided becoming an investor because you simply don't know where to get started. Once you have determined that you are in the right position to begin investing, you want to consider the following based on your short and long-term financial goals.

Retirement Funds

One of the first investments people make is toward some form of a retirement fund, either a 401(k), individual retirement account (IRA), or a tax-free retirement account (TFRA) plan. It's very likely that if you're married and your spouse is working that they have the opportunity to put a dedicated amount of their pay into a 401(k) retirement fund.

Most workplaces offer 401(k) plans, and some will match your contributions, meaning you can get even bigger returns the more you invest, with certain limitations. A 401(k) is not the same as a pension plan, so be careful that you understand what you have. You should sit down with your partner to discuss this plan. If your partner doesn't know the details about their retirement fund, they can contact their HR department to learn about their specific plan.

A 401(k) gives you an easy way to start saving for retirement, and there are a few ways you can contribute to this fund to ensure that you have enough when retirement comes around. For most, you can have money deposited directly into your 401(k) plan from each paycheck. Most 401(k) plans will only let you add $19,500 a year to your account if you are under 50 and $26,000 a year if you are over 50. There are other types of employer-sponsored retirement plans such as 403(b), 457(b), and thrift savings plans (TSPs).

If you or your spouse don't have a 401(k) and it isn't offered at your or their place of work, you can still set up a retirement fund. If you started investing aggressively early on with your 401(k), you might find that you have maxed out your benefits, and contributing to an alternative retirement plan may be a good idea as well. Traditional IRAs and Roth IRAs are two options to consider.

IRAs can be set up easily through your local bank or a brokerage firm. These accounts have limitations on how much you can contribute a year. With a traditional IRA, you can only add $6,000 a year to an IRA account if you are under 50 and $7,000 a year if you are over 50. There are also limitations based on whether or not you or your spouse already has a 401(k) through an employer.

With a Roth IRA, yearly contributions are based on your modified adjusted gross income. The more you make, the less you can invest. The key difference between these two account types is when taxes are taken out. With Roth IRAs, the money you invest at the time is taxed, but you are not taxed when you begin withdrawing from the account.

With traditional IRAs, you are not taxed on the money you invest at the time of investment, but you are taxed on the money you withdraw from the accounts. This may sound like a great option, except having to pay taxes on this money when you are retired can leave you with a misrepresentation of how much money you actually have access to.

For those who are self-employed or entrepreneurs, you can establish a Simplified Employee Pension (SEP) IRA, Solo 401(k), or Savings Incentive Match Plan for Employees (SIMPLE) IRA retirement account. These retirement plans can be more complex to set up yourself, and it's best to discuss your options with a professional financial adviser so you understand your limitations and options.

Managing these funds will require more effort on your part as you are the sole decision-maker and have a greater pool of investment options to choose from. Many self-employed retirement plans have fewer regulations on when you can withdraw and have added benefits of profit sharing. If you're planning on starting a side hustle or your own business, you want to consider investing in one of these plans.

Mutual Funds

Mutual funds are a basket of investments where you buy a share of the fund. This share is an investment into all the fund's holdings of securities such as stocks and bonds—for each share you buy, it grants you another piece of ownership.

Mutual funds are managed by a fund manager who is in charge of monitoring the performance of the companies the fund is based on. This investment option allows you to diversify your portfolio through one investment and lowers the risk of you losing all of your investment.

This doesn't mean there is no risk. Mutual funds can be a higher-risk investment because the value can fluctuate and even fall, but even with the liquidity, any losses that occur can be redeemed over time. For beginners, mutual funds can be a sensible way to become an investor as they have a low entry cost.

Target-date mutual funds are retirement-driven mutual funds. These investments are typically made with your retirement date in mind. These are automatically invested in as a part of your retirement plan. The further away your retirement date is, the more likely that your investment will go toward various stocks. As your retirement year approaches, these investments will shift into bonds since they carry a much lower risk but still allow you to grow your money.

Other types of mutual funds include:

- **Money market funds**: These investments have lower risk because they are required to be high-quality US corporations, and they must be issued by the local, state, and federal governments.
- **Bond funds**: These have more risk because they are meant to yield a high return, but there are various types of bonds that drastically vary in the risk attached to them.
- **Stock funds**: Stock funds come in various forms, and each comes with a different method of growing your money.

Before investing in any type of mutual fund, it's important that you read up on the company's prospectus. This document will reveal vital information about the company objectives, risk, performance, expenses, and history. Any company offering investment opportunities is required to file a prospectus and make shareholder reports available. If you cannot find this information, do not invest in the mutual fund.

You can begin investing in a mutual fund by purchasing shares from the fund itself or through a broker of the fund. Keep in mind that fund fees, dividends, and shared values can change over time and without much warning. You are able to sell back your shares to the fund whenever you choose and will often receive a payment within a week of the sale.

Index Funds

Index funds are similar to mutual funds, with the exception that they track the market index. Market index refers to a set of investments that make up a portion of the market. You may have heard of the Standard & Poor's 500 index (S&P 500). This is a market index that is made up of the stock of 500 of the largest companies in the US. The S&P 500 index fund will look at how the S&P 500 is performing and will mimic what it is doing. The index fund will then invest in stocks of the same companies that make up the S&P 500.

Like mutual funds, you're buying a larger section of the market with one investment, but it takes a more passive approach than mutual funds. Index funds are not typically professionally managed as they simply track the market and make investments based on the ups and downs. You still are putting your money into various funds, making it an easy way to diversify your portfolio quickly. These investments are ideal for those with a lower risk tolerance and are much more valuable as you hold on to them for the long term.

Index funds can be great for individuals who want to begin investing but have little money to begin investing with. While many brokerage firms will require a minimum to begin an investment, some firms, like Fidelity, will allow you to invest without a minimal requirement. Index funds also incur fewer fees because they don't require the assessment or research like mutual funds. Since this will follow the traditional index, much of the behind the scenes work is already done. This means these investments tend to do better than their market indexes.

Exchange-Traded Funds

Exchange-traded funds (ETFs) are similar to index funds. They track the market index, but they also tend to have lower fees. ETFs track a set of equities, stocks of an industry, or an entire index.

When you buy an ETF, you can buy into a basket of equities which will help diversify your portfolio like an index fund. The main difference between an ETF and an index fund is that ETFs are traded frequently throughout the day in the same way that traditional stocks are traded. At any time during the day, the investment minimum can be under one hundred dollars or a few hundred dollars.

The main benefit from ETFs is that although they are bought and sold like stock, most brokers do not charge a commission for trading them which you get charged with trading individual stocks.

Some ETF brokers to consider include:

- TD Ameritrade
- E-Trade Financial Corporation
- Fidelity Investments
- Ally Invest
- Charles Schwab

There's an App For That

As with most things in the world, there are plenty of investment apps that can help you get started with investing and growing your money. These apps will let you begin with a minimal start, and some even provide bonus periods where you will be rewarded with some free money to begin your investment when you sign up. Many of the brokers listed in the ETF section also have apps that will let you begin investing and keep an eye on your wealth from anywhere.

Acorn and Stash are two beginner investments apps that will let you learn as you grow your investments. Acorn lets you invest your leftover change from purchases. The change is put toward a diversified portfolio and is managed by a robo adviser system. You just need to link a debit or credit card to your Acorn account.

Every purchase you make is then rounded up to the nearest dollar, and once you have a total of just five dollars in your round-up collection, the money gets invested. There is a monthly service fee of one dollar. You also have an option to start an individual retirement account, which will cost two dollars a month.

These IRA accounts come with some perks that you will want to take advantage of if you are unsure whether to start with a standard account or an IRA account.

Robo Advisers

Robo advisers make it easy for anyone to begin investing without having to know all the ins and outs of the markets or investment jargon. While it's certainly advisable that you gain a basic understanding of where your money is going and what to expect in the form of returns, many people would much rather someone else handle their investment options.

Robo advisers are automated services that will invest for you. They use a special algorithm that takes into consideration your risk tolerance and investment goals to put your money in the most effective place so you can achieve those goals.

What makes these services appealing to beginners is not just the ways of use but also the lower fees. Many services do not require a minimum balance to begin investing. There is also a low annual fee that is not more than .5 percent of your account balance.

Using a robo adviser is a great way for you to understand the investment process better and allow you to learn as you invest with less risk. While these services will do a bulk of the work for you, you don't want to be completely hands-off. I advise you always keep an eye on where your money is going and how much it is growing.

Testamentary Trusts

A testamentary trust should be created by you and your partner if you are married or have children. If you're not married, you should still establish a testamentary trust for your wealth after you are gone.

A testamentary trust is created based on a last will and testament. This type of trust establishes how assets are to be distributed and managed after one passes and, technically, is not created until after death. If you have younger children, it's a good idea to include a testamentary trust in your will. If you have older children, a testamentary trust can ensure your children (and not their spouses) have sole access to the inheritance.

Testamentary trusts can protect assets after death and allow you (if your spouse includes a testamentary trust) or your children if you suddenly pass, to have funds available to them. Keep in mind, though, that legal fees around these trusts can become quite costly. It's worth looking into with your partner to determine if a testamentary trust would be financially wise for your family.

Also, keep in mind Bonnie from our earlier example. She established funds with her children's name on the account as a secondary account holder. While she was living, she was taking care of the taxes from these investments and simplified the process for her children to gain access to these accounts. You can look at your options for doing something similar for your children, grandchildren, and other family members.

Chapter Highlights

- Understand how investing can help you achieve long-term financial goals.
- Determine if this is the right time for you to begin investing. Remember, if your debt is paid off and you have an emergency fund, there should be nothing stopping you from starting to invest.
- Begin a retirement fund, and look at what options you have through your or your spouse's place of employment. Always look at your options and ask questions.
- Establish your risk tolerance and then narrow down which investment options are best suited for you.

Chapter 7

Getting Out of Debt

"*Debt erases freedom more surely than anything else.*" – Merryn Somerset Webb

If you have debt, your first priority is to eliminate it. You may think that having a few credit cards open with a few hundred or thousands of dollars on them is no big deal. You're probably well aware of how the interest rates of these accounts are going to waste your money month after month. If you take a moment to review your debt, you will discover that a majority of what you pay each month, especially if you are only paying the minimum amount, goes toward interest rates. Those minimum monthly payments are barely bringing down your total owing.

This is why so many people get stuck with an endless amount of debt, and despite them paying every month, the balance barely budges. Debt is a heavy burden, but even with hundreds or even thousands of dollars of debt, there is hope.

Jessica, fresh out of college, had over $100,000 in student loan debt. Her first job barely paid $40,000 a year, so she knew if she wanted to get rid of her debt, she was going to have to do so aggressively. She lived below her means, picked up side jobs whenever she could, and was able to pay off that $100,000 in seven years, a feat that would take others at least twice as long.

Linda and her husband had a total of $70,000 worth of credit card debt, car loans, and medical bills. They constantly fought about paying it off, and the stress was beginning to strain their marriage. They sat down and came up with an effective

repayment strategy that would allow them to pay off the debt in six years. With some cuts to their nonessentials and a fine-tuned spending plan, they were able to pay off that debt in just three years. While your debt may seem impossible now, there are ways you can lower it and even eliminate it completely in less time than you think.

There are plenty of approaches to getting out of debt, and if you are married or in a partnership, this is something both of you need to be on the same page with. Before you can gain financial independence, start planning for your future seriously, or take control of your money, you need to eliminate your debt.

How Debt Compounds

Just as interest compounds over the years when you put money into a savings account, so does the interest that gets added on to your debts. Unfortunately, it feels like debt interest compounds at a much faster rate than our savings or investments. This compounding catches people off guard, so even those who have a clear understanding of their finances can find themselves in a mountain of debt.

There are also the great low-interest time periods in which we make big purchases and assume we can pay the debt off before this benefit period ends. Instead, we often make the minimum payments each month, and after the no-interest time is up, high rates are applied, and it's as though we never paid a cent toward lowering the balance.

Many people get sucked into the idea that they won't have to worry about more debt accumulation. While a no-interest-fee promotion can be worth taking advantage of, it's only beneficial if you can pay off the balance before the interest takes effect.

We get into debt because of one simple truth—at some point we spend more than we bring in. The number of credit cards you have may have helped fuel these habits. This spend-now-pay-later philosophy has allowed many of us to think we can afford things that are well out of our means.

Debt can become overwhelming, but this does not mean it can't be eliminated. Even if you have felt like you've lived your entire life in debt, you can slowly begin to rid your debt one account at a time.

To help you track your debt repayment, I've created a Debt Repayment Tracker that you can download as part of the free Budget Planner Bundle at www.zoem adden.com.

Taking Control of Your Debt

The first step to getting rid of your debt is to understand how much you owe, individually and as a couple. Many people use their credit cards far more than they realize and rarely check their balances. They just look at how much they should pay that month and make a payment. To create an effective debt-repayment plan, you need to take inventory of how much debt you have.

Unfortunately, there is no easy or fun way to get out of debt, but if you want financial freedom, it's essential. This means you may have to make a few sacrifices and cut back on some nonessentials. We get short-lived satisfaction from spending on the things we want and rarely consider the long-term reward of paying off our debt by not spending.

Create a realistic debt repayment plan. Paying off debt is going to discourage you because you are going to want to spend more than you put toward your debt, but this is going to leave you a prisoner of your debt for longer. While a nice vacation or upgraded television may be well deserved and desired, spending large amounts of money is only going to hinder your progress. As you begin to pay off your debt, the following will help you make progress and stay committed.

This Is a Family Effort

Getting rid of your debt will require everyone in your household to be on the same page. If you're married, in a serious relationship, or have kids, everyone needs to be aware of the cuts you will be making and be supportive of eliminating the debt. You and your partner will need to sit down and create a debt repayment plan together. They may not be aware of how much debt you both have accumulated over the years, and they may not see the urgency to get rid of it. Working as a team will make the process easier, and you'll see your debt diminish quicker if you are all working together.

Paying off debt will require cutting back on some of the things you and your family may have grown accustomed to, such as a premium cable package, eating out, and having multiple snacks available in the home. You might not have to eliminate all these things entirely, but you will need to be more mindful of how much money is going toward these luxuries. You and your family will need to adjust, but it's important that you discuss these changes with the household before implementing them and putting everyone into shock.

Having a family meeting is a great idea to bring up some of the changes that will be occurring and get their input on some other ways you all can save a little more. When everyone in the home feels like they are participating and being a part of the process, they will be more eager to make changes.

Know where to look for free and fun activities to do in your area with your kids or as a family. Plan special nights and day trips, like movie nights at home and taking nature walks, allowing you all to enjoy time together without being bored or feeling like you are missing out. Get your family's input on things you can do together.

Some ways you can save money together include:

Make meals at home together.

- Create a grocery list together, and ask your kids to help find coupons and look for stores with the best deals on the items you need.

- Find free activities through your local community newsletter or website.

- Create a family side business together.
- Shop at bargain stores for clothes.
- Have theme nights.
- Start a new hobby together.
- Exercise together.
- Explore the outdoors and your community more.
- Create a family budget together.
- Create a vision board for what everyone in the family would like to do if there was a little extra money in the budget to do these things.
- Make gifts or crafts for neighbors, other family members, and one another for birthdays and holidays instead of spending money.

Finally, come up with an easy way to save more than just money, such as cutting back on water waste or electricity use. You can even set up a recycling system and exchange some of those recyclables for some extra money. You will save money, and everyone in the house plays a part.

Dealing With Discouragement

One thing you want to acknowledge before implementing a debt repayment plan is that paying off your debt isn't going to happen overnight. I don't want to discourage you but I have be honest about the fact that it can take years to eliminate debt completely. While you may have easily racked up thousands of dollars of debt in a short time, getting rid of it is not going to be as quick. It's important to accept this fact so you don't abandon your debt repayment plan because it's taking a long time to make it go away.

Keep in mind that while you're making cuts to certain things in your budget to reallocate money to go toward your debt, you need to ensure that you're making room for activities that you enjoy. The main reason so many people neglect repaying their debt is that when they start trying to lower it, there is little left for fun things. They begin to feel deprived and discouraged. To keep you motivated, it's vital you have a big long-term goal in mind for when your debt is paid off.

You might be discouraged right from the start when you realize how long paying off your debt is going to take. Try not to focus on how long it will take. Instead, focus on dwindling down your debt a little at a time, and remind yourself of how you are going to feel each time you bring down your debt a little more and eventually pay it off.

Every three or four months, check in with your progress. This is to ensure that you are staying on track with your repayment plan based on your current income. Then look over what is and is not working for you. Are there additional ways you might be able to cut back to bring down your debt a little more?

Debt Snowball Method

You will come across many suggestions and methods for paying off debt, but the most common is referred to as the snowball method. When you have multiple debts, you do not want to just make the minimum payment on each one. This will only keep you stuck in debt for much longer. Instead, you need to choose one to pay off first while paying the minimum balance on the others.

Once you have one debt paid off, you reallocate the money you were putting toward that debt to another debt. Then you continue to make those same payments, plus the minimum monthly payments you have been making until that debt is paid off. Then, again, you reallocate that money to the next debt.

This method is effective because you work toward paying off one debt entirely at a time while bringing the others down slightly. You don't have to worry about switching up your budget. All the money that is going toward your debt repayment will remain the same, but as one debt gets paid off, you will be able to bring down the next account faster.

Applying the snowball method to a debt scenario could look something like this:

- You have credit card debt that equals $7,000 with combined interest rates of 10%. Keep in mind, for this example, that you will add up the total amount of credit card debt and the total interest paid as a whole, not for each individual account. You may have some cards that have the lowest interest rates.
- You have student loan debt of $15,000 with combined interest rates of 6%. Each semester of school you participate in leaves you with a new student loan to cover. You'll add up your total student loan debt but put a portion of your overall monthly student loan payment toward each individual loan.
- You have a car loan of $11,000 with an interest rate of 3%.

With the snowball method, you will first pay off your credit card debt, as it has the lowest balance. You'll determine how much money you are putting toward your debt repayment. Remember that you need this to be greater than paying the minimum balance on your accounts. When you begin your repayment, you will put all your extra money for your debt toward your credit cards while making the minimum payments on your other debts.

Once you have your credit cards paid off, you reallocate the money you were using to pay off the credit cards to the next lowest balance. In this example, that is the car loan. Once that is paid off, you put all your money toward paying off your student loans.

You can also apply the same principle to pay off the accounts that have the highest interest rates first, then work your way through your debt to your lowest interest rate. So for this example, you would begin by paying off your credit cards, then student loans, and then move on to your car loan.

You'll need to choose the best approach to paying off the debt that works for you. Each approach, either focusing on the smallest balance or the highest interest rate, will allow you to accelerate your debt repayment goals.

Both methods make sense, and each can help you cut your total amount owing, but until everything is paid, you will still accumulate more debt due to interest rates. If you haven't done so already, reach out to the company you have the debts with to try to get a lower interest rate.

There are a few things to keep in mind when choosing which debt to tackle first.

1. **Paying off the smallest debt first can help build momentum** and keep you motivated to tackle the rest of your debt. So many of us rely on instant gratification, and the sooner we can see that our debt is being taken care of, the more we believe in our ability to get rid of it entirely.

2. **Paying off the highest interest account first can save you in the long term but may also take longer to pay off.** You will need to make a much larger monthly payment on high-interest accounts, and this can be hard to do when you are also paying off multiple other accounts.

3. **You might want to start off with paying off a few of your smaller accounts first** and then tackle your high-interest debts next. This can help you eliminate debt, and once you have two or three accounts off the table, you have the extra money to put toward your high-interest accounts without having to figure out where the additional money will come from.

4. **Understand how much interest your accounts will add to your debt as you go**. Obviously, high-interest accounts will add more, but if you have a handful of other accounts with lower interest rates, when added together, these lower interest accounts may add just as much to your debt.

5. When it comes to credit card debt, **it's important that you are not using these cards for any additional purchases**. You can't pay off a debt if you are still adding to it. Until you are debt-free, avoid adding any new debts to your name or contributing to the debt you already have.

There are a few exceptions that should be made when paying off debt. For example, you signed up for a credit card to make a big purchase like a new appliance for the kitchen. One of the special conditions of using this card for these purchases was that you wouldn't pay any interest for a given number of months.

You want to pay this card off first. Even though it may not be the smallest amount and certainly does not have the highest interest rate, you want to clear this debt before it starts adding to your overall debt owing. Leaving this account to pay off later because it currently isn't adding interest to the balance can result in large debt. It's better to pay this off first before the special time period runs out so you are not at risk of adding more to your debt.

You can download a Debt Snowball Worksheet to help you track your debt repayment if you choose to use this method. The worksheet is part of the free Budget Planner Bundle available at www.zoemadden.com.

Other Get-Out-Of Debt Options

Consolidating Debts

If you have a lot of high-interest debt, it can be a smart idea to try to roll all these accounts into one lower interest rate account. This can make your debt more manageable and can help you save more in repayment in the long term. There are pros and cons of this repayment option, and it isn't for everyone. You should also not consider a debt consolidation option if your debt accounts for more than half your income.

While debt consolidation can help you get rid of debt faster, it's not always the best option. If you do not first address poor spending habits prior to debt consolidation, you run a much greater risk of missing payments or running your debt up once again. Debt consolidation also will not help if it still does not provide you with an easier way to pay off your debt. For example, if you are still unable to make monthly payments on time, even with the lower interest rate of a debt consolidation loan, this option is only going to impact your credit negatively.

Negotiating With Creditors

As we mentioned earlier, one of your first steps to eliminating debt should be getting a lower interest rate on your accounts. Another option, if you are seriously struggling with repaying any debt, is to try to negotiate a lower payoff amount. If you have defaulted on some of your accounts, this can be a viable option, though you do not want to purposely miss payments for it to be a consideration.

Many companies are eager to get their money back, and if you are able to pay a large amount, which will be a majority of what you owe, you might be able to work out some type of arrangement to do so. With this approach, you pay a portion of what you owe as a one-time payment and then have the account closed out. For example, if you have a credit card bill that you owe $3,000 on, you might be able to come to a debt agreement where you pay $2,000 of the amount. The rest gets written off, and the account is then closed.

Debt Relief

Different debt relief options can make it easier and possible to wipe out debt, but there are some that will only cause you to get further into debt. Many debt relief offers can be a scam, leaving you with a bigger debt than you started with.

Debt relief programs that are legit will be beneficial to help you with unsecured debts, like credit card debt and personal loans. If you are unable to pay these debts off within five years, or your debt payments are greater than half your income, a debt relief program can be an answer to your debt problem.

Before you agree to any type of debt relief program, you need to verify that it is a legitimate program. Once verified, you need to be sure to understand all the agreements. Know what you qualify for. Are you getting lower interest rates, different payment dates, or a lower balance on what you owe? Then be sure you're aware of all the fees you will be paying. Some relief payments will only require you to make a lump sum payment without any additional fees.

You also need to know what accounts are being paid and how much of it is being paid. Some relief methods will only focus on repaying one account; others will help you consolidate your debt and pay each of the creditors through your agreement. This often means that the debt is being transferred to a settlement company that will take care of the account until it is paid off or brought up to date.

If you know you can pay your debt within five years (if you cut back on your spending), then you want to try to erase your debt yourself. Going through a debt relief program can reflect negatively on your credit score.

Bankruptcy

Bankruptcy is not a fun experience and puts your credit on hold for seven to ten years. You won't be able to make big purchases that require a credit check if you file for bankruptcy. This option should be an absolute last resort but might be a necessary move for those who have an unmanageable and overwhelming amount of debt.

If you have thoroughly considered all your debt repayment options and have no way to cut back more on your spending and make payments, even if they were reduced, then bankruptcy might be your only option to be free of your debt.

Bankruptcy can only be used for eliminating many unsecured debts through Chapter 7 liquidation. It can take up to three months for all accounts to be cleared but will not help you with student loan debt, back taxes owed, or unpaid child support. Be mindful of cosigned accounts. If you have a cosigner on an account, the person who cosigned the debt will then be responsible for it, and they should be made aware of this.

Also, be aware that some bankruptcies can take your property or other assets to help pay back some of your creditors. This will vary from state to state, so be sure you understand the severity of the consequences and the risk of losing more than just your debt through bankruptcy.

Bankruptcy is not always going to help you out. If you find yourself returning to poor spending habits after you have filed for bankruptcy, don't just think you can file again. You have to wait eight years before you will be permitted to file for another bankruptcy.

One of the requirements many people have to complete for their bankruptcy is to complete a financial course that teaches you better money habits so you can avoid getting stuck with too much debt again.

What Not To Do When Paying Off Debt

Debt repayment is stressful and can cloud your judgment when it comes to making the best decisions to eliminate your debt. You will feel pressured to obtain money faster to pay off debts, and this can lead to huge devastation. While debt is stressful, there are some things you do not want to do, no matter how many times a creditor calls seeking a payment, including:

- **Do not skip paying on secured debts.** Missing a payment on a secured debt will result in the loss of collateral. For example, if you skip car payments, you will eventually lose your car. If you have to choose between a secured debt or unsecured debt, always pay the secured debts first.

- **Do not put your home up for collateral.** Many people borrow against the equity of their home, which puts their home at risk of foreclosure. Doing this turns your unsecured debts into a secured debt that you can't miss making a payment on. Remember, unsecured debts can be wiped clean through various methods, including bankruptcy, but your secured debts can't.

- **Do not touch your retirement funds**, not even your workplace retirement plans. This is a mistake many people make. They borrow money from their retirement to pay off their debts and make their retirement goals unachievable.

- No matter how many calls you get, **never make a choice about debt repayment until you have taken the time to research and understand all your options**. Making a choice just because you are feeling pressured by creditors will cause you to make a poor decision.

Staying Out of Debt

Some debt is inevitable. When you purchase a new home, it's very likely you will have a mortgage, which for many is unavoidable if they ever want to make homeownership a reality. Other debts can be completely avoided, like credit card debt. Getting out of debt and remaining debt-free is not just about gaining financial literacy; it's about adopting a different lifestyle.

To keep yourself out of debt, you need to prioritize your money wants and needs. When you rid your debt, it can be easy to fall back into poor spending habits. It's OK to indulge in things every once in a while if you want to ensure you are spending your money on the more meaningful things in your life.

Credit Cards Are Not for Emergencies

Credit card debt quickly accumulates because most people have the perception of credit cards as an easy way to buy now and worry about paying later. While having one or two credit card accounts can help keep your credit score up, these should not be treated as an extended bank account.

You should never use your credit card to make a purchase you can't immediately pay off. For example, if you don't have the funds to buy that new smartphone, do not be tempted to put it on a charge card with the idea that you can afford the monthly payments instead of paying for the phone fully upon purchase. Just because you can afford the monthly payments doesn't make it a wise choice. You will end up paying hundreds more for that phone due to interest fees.

Whenever you use your credit card to make a purchase, you should only do so when you know you can pay off the balance. Don't fall into the trap of using your credit cards for emergencies. This is why you have set up an emergency fund and have other accounts dedicated for when sudden expenses occur. Using your credit cards for emergencies is going to add up to unmanageable debt.

Seek Help Before It Spirals Out of Control

Don't wait to get help. If you're struggling to stay on budget, make payments, or use good spending habits, ask for professional guidance before it gets worse. If you're struggling to make payments, it's much better to act early than to wait until you begin missing payments. You need to be honest with yourself and what you struggle with when it comes to money. It may be that your thoughts and perceptions about money have a deeply rooted negative attachment to something from your past.

Addressing your mindset and belief system around money with the help of a professional will lead you to a more financially freeing life.

Chapter Highlights

- Understand your debts and categorize them as secured or unsecured.
- Identify how much money you can afford to put toward your debt repayment.
- Choose a repayment option that will streamline your efforts so you can pay off your debt quickly.
- Be clear about why it's important to pay off these debts and the freedoms you'll have once they are paid off.
- Know what spending habits you need to keep an eye on so that you don't find yourself in debt again.
- Don't forget you can download your free Budget Planner Bundle at www.zoemadden.com. The bundle includes both a Debt Repayment Tracker and a Debt Snowball Worksheet.

Chapter 8

Financial Goals

"All I ask is the chance to prove that money can't make me happy." – Spike Milligan.

Where do you want to be with your finances? How can you get there? Whether you're married or single, it's important to have financial goals. They can be personal goals or goals for your household. Either way, these goals lay the foundation for your budget planning as they give you something tangible to work towards. Importantly, a good financial goal will provide the motivation needed for you to stick to your budget.

Unfortunately, many people allow their limitations to keep them from setting goals or achieving what they are capable of. They allow these limitations to be barriers, and this doesn't just impact their finances. Chances are, if you're hesitant to set financial goals for yourself, you are also hesitant to set goals in other areas of your life.

While it may not be clear to you now, you can turn your limitation into a powerful force that will push you to not only set goals and crush them but let this success create the momentum you need to fuel other changes you desire in your life. This type of thinking and empowerment can be applied to any situation and any transformation you seek.

Why Set Financial Goals?

Setting goals is more than just outlining what and how you will achieve something. It requires adopting the right mindset to achieve those goals. Without the right mindset, it's very hard to reach your goals, big or small.

Goals should be set for the short to long term. Sticking to a budget and having an emergency fund are short-term financial goals to work toward. Paying off debt, saving for a down payment on a car or home are mid-term goals, and things like retirement savings or college funds are long-term goals.

You need to have the right motivation to push you to stay committed, and this can be a combination of internal and external factors. We love instant gratification, and rewarding good spending habits and achieving small milestones on our way to bigger goals will keep us on track.

Solely relying on external rewards for motivation will eventually lose its luster though. You may be able to convince yourself to set a little extra aside in your savings account and reward yourself with a nice bubble bath every once in a while, but soon you will need to rely on your own internal willpower to push through the temptations and obstacles.

Intrinsic motivation is the key to goal achievement. It's what we need to rely on to establish better money habits. We use it as a way to encourage ourselves and to instill a belief in ourselves that we can accomplish what we set out to accomplish.

Unlike external motivations, internal motivation is not a one-and-done reward. The more you can turn to your self-motivation to do what you need to do, the easier it will be to turn these things into habits that you no longer have to question or think about doing. They become a part of who you are.

How we spend and save are connected to key habits, which are internally and externally triggered by our thoughts and mindset. We can reach for and accomplish our most intimidating goals by addressing our mindset about money, spending, saving, and financial success. Our mindset can be changed, and this is achieved through proper motivation.

Listing goals gets you thinking about your possibilities. Setting goals requires you to consider the effort you will need to put into taking action to achieve those goals.

Setting goals, however, is not about what you gain or accomplish. When you take action on achieving goals, the process will shift to who you are becoming. This is where the power of setting goals lies—not in the actions you do but the person those actions transform you into. This allows you to push your limits to recognize how much more you can learn and grow. You'll find yourself seeking out opportunities instead of waiting for them to appear, and stepping outside your comfort zone so you can grow into a better version of yourself.

Please try this even if you think you might fail. Failure is an essential part of growth. If you don't stumble a few times along the way, you won't find the most effective way to accomplish your goals. Even if you don't achieve your goals exactly as you first intended, there are still lessons that will provide you with opportunities to do better next time.

When it comes to our finances, we can apply this try-and-fail mentality in many ways. If you've started investing, this will apply throughout your investing journey. If you're trying to adopt better spending habits, like combating impulse spending, you will try different methods until you find the right one that sticks.

There are plenty of stories about people who have this rich mindset who have overcome great adversity and obstacles to accomplish the impossible. You may know people with this mindset or have read stories or seen articles of people going after and reaching their biggest dreams despite their limitations. There are people crawling up mountains and touring across the US in their wheelchairs to inspire others to work with what they have instead of fighting against it. There are people beating cancer and going on to complete marathons and ironman competitions—individuals who, despite being told over and over again that their dreams are impossible, found a way to achieve them.

Thousands of people overcome great obstacles. Becoming financially independent will be just a small hill you climb that will lead to reaching for more.

Financial Goals to Get Started With

We can apply this reach mindset to achieve many vital financial goals such as:

- **Build up an emergency fund**: Creating an emergency fund can be a part of your short-term financial goals, but it has long-term benefits. When an unexpected emergency comes up, you already have savings that will lessen the financial blow. Your emergency fund will allow you to continue with your long-term investment plans and give you an alternate fund to use instead of having to withdraw from a retirement fund or investment account.

- **Eliminate debt**: Create and stick with a debt repayment plan so you can have more control over your finances. We covered debt-repayment options in the last chapter, and it should be a top priority financial goal. It's difficult to achieve your other financial goals when you have a pile of debt looming over you and the majority of your income goes to just making the minimum payments.

  When you're debt-free, you will have more money to put toward your savings, investment, and the things you value most. There is a great deal of anxiety and stress over having debt, and eliminating this debt will also eliminate the extra stress.

- **Plan for retirement**: You can never start planning for retirement too early no matter how old you are. Set up a retirement plan, one where you may even be able to retire early. Many people neglect the importance of having a retirement fund despite it being a top concern for a majority of people.

There are many things that might keep you from working as you get older. Without a retirement account set up, this can be devastating. Also, you've spent your whole life working. As you get older, you are going to want to spend your time doing more of the things that fulfill you, like spending time with grandkids. Your values will shift, and a retirement fund will allow you to make the shift in your lifestyle.

The longer you wait to set up a retirement fund, the harder it will be to achieve your retirement financial goals. If you start early, it will allow you to build up your investment portfolio so you won't have to work so hard to add to your fund later to have enough for retirement.

- **Obtain the right coverage**: Research and set up insurance plans that cover contingencies. Insurance can be a tricky topic. If you don't have an insurance policy, you need to get one. If you do have one, you need to review it to make sure it covers enough should anything happen.

  You also need to check you aren't paying too much by comparing companies regularly. There are some key types of insurance you should be focused on: life insurance, health insurance, and auto insurance. Your life insurance policy should be term life insurance because it tends to cost less. Health insurance policies are complex, and many pay high copayments and are deductible. If you are in good health and have an established medical emergency fund, it may be wiser to have a high deductible health insurance plan to cover the difference for medical expenses.
  If you have a history of being a safe driver, you may be paying too much for auto insurance. Consider reviewing what your auto insurance entails and see if you can downgrade to a more affordable policy.

You might want to consider seeking out professional advice on the best types of insurance you should be purchasing. This can help you determine what life insurance policy makes sense for you, whether you can get a lower price on auto insurance, and if your health insurance policy fits your health needs.

- **Minimize your spending**: Embrace your ability to live on less than you earn. Learning to live under your means is a smart financial goal. When you adjust your spending habits so that you cover your essentials and have a little fun money while also having more to put away for savings and investments, you will be better off. While you can always find ways to increase your income, your money won't go far if you do not first learn how to live on less. Learning to live on less is not about depriving yourself. It is about being able to put your income to better use.
- **Establish a second income stream**: Having more than one stream of income not only makes reaching your other financial goals more feasible, it gives you security for the long term. Whether you are working or relying on your partner's employment as a main source of income, these jobs are not guaranteed.

  There are many unfortunate events that can leave you or your partner without work, and finding another place of employment may not be easy or pay the same. Having an extra income will give you more financial security, even if it is just a few hundred dollars a month. This extra income will allow you to put more into savings or paying off debt, but it also means you are not relying on one single income.

  If you have been used to being a stay-at-home mom and want to contribute more financially or feel more secure about your financial independence, you need to create an income stream for yourself. This can be a variety of side hustles or small business ideas.

Starting just one small income stream can lead to many more income opportunities. A quick internet search will help you find various ideas to get started with that require little to no upfront investments.

Setting SMART Financial Goals

Your financial goals should align with what you define as success. These goals should also work with your other personal goals as many of these personal goals tend to have a financial impact backing. For example, a common personal goal is to lose weight or be healthier. This can directly impact your finances as you can save a decent amount of money by cutting out junk foods and cooking more at home. Another example is wanting to start your own business.

Your financial goals will directly relate to these goals, as they will allow you to bring in your own income and influence other aspects of your life.

SMART goal-setting methods are a popular way to be clear and concise about what you want to accomplish. With the SMART method, you set specific, measurable, attainable, realistic, and time-bound goals. While many people recommend these methods for achieving all types of personal and professional goals, the same method can be applied to your financial goals.

Specific

Goals that are specific leave little room for misunderstandings or making excuses. Saying you want to have a savings account does not give you clarity on what you want. Everyone wants to have some money in savings, but if you manage to set up savings with only five dollars, technically, you have achieved your goal. Chances are, you want much more than five dollars and will need to have a precise amount to ensure you continue to save until you reach that desired amount.

Specific goals will tell you exactly what you want to accomplish with your finances. The more detail this is, the better idea you have on how to set up an action plan to accomplish this. Your specific goal should not only say what you want to accomplish but how or why this will improve your life.

For example, *I want to pay off my credit card debt so that I can have more money to put toward saving for my kid's college fund.* This clarifies the specific goal of paying off your credit card debt and the reason it's important for you to do this.

Measurable

A measurable goal is a goal you can track. Only through tracking will you see if you are making the progress you need to be making and sticking to your action plan. With financial goals, measurable will often be a dollar amount. For example, you want to invest $5,000 into a retirement account.

Achievable

Your goal must be achievable, and you must decide how you are going to achieve it. This part of the goal-setting process also needs to be specific. Based on your income, your goal must fit into your budget, and you must state how it does.

For example, you want to save for a down payment for a new car. You can accomplish this because your current income allows you to set aside two hundred dollars a month to save for the car.

Realistic

I encourage setting big goals because I firmly believe that if you want to achieve something enough, you will find a way. However, I don't want to imply that goals will be accomplished based on sheer luck. It takes effort to turn a goal into reality, and you have to be willing and able to put in this effort. There are also goals that are nice to work toward but may not be the best to set for yourself when other financial issues need to be accomplished.

By all means, dream big. If you want to become the wealthiest person in the world, go ahead and aim high. But first, let's start with the steps you need to take to get there. A more realistic goal on your way to becoming the wealthiest person is paying off your debt or making wise investments. These are within your reach and could potentially one day lead you to bigger financial gains.

You don't want to set a goal that is not achievable based on your current financial standings. This is not meant to discourage you. Setting a goal that you can't reach with your current income is going to set you up for disappointment. If you can't realistically accomplish the goal, reconsider the goal you are setting. If you want to pay off your debt but don't have the financial means to dedicate to paying it off, your financial goal might be better if it was to create a second income stream.

Just because you can't work toward one goal immediately doesn't mean it isn't worth working toward. You do need to consider what resources you have available and what other factors will support or hinder your efforts.

Time-Bound

If you don't attach a deadline or an "accomplish by" date, you will tend to drag your feet on getting started, and therefore will most likely never achieve what you want. Just as you would have deadlines for work projects and as your kids have due dates for homework assignments, you need to set and stick with a deadline to achieve your financial goals.

This "accomplish by" date needs to be realistic. Unless you have a big inheritance coming or just won the lottery, saving a million dollars in your retirement fund in just five years is probably not going to happen. Be realistic about what you can currently afford and the restrictions you face. Even something like creating and sticking to a budget, which feels like it should be accomplished in a month, will need to be reworked to ensure it is the best budget for your long-term goals. You want to set a deadline, but you also need to be honest with yourself and your abilities to meet those deadlines based on what you have control over.

With any type of goal, the biggest issue about setting deadlines for yourself is that it is very easy to let the deadline approach and the goal not be achieved. This is why your goal also needs to be measurable and realistic. By taking these two factors into consideration, you can estimate how long it should take you to achieve your goal.

For example, if you have credit card debt that amounts to $10,000, and you establish a budget that allows you to contribute $1,000 monthly to your debt-repayment plan, when you factor in interest rates, it should take you about 12 to 14 months to pay off.

Reviewing Your Financial Progress

Once you have your SMART financial goals established, it's not enough to just start taking action. You need to set aside time each week, month, and year to review your progress, reevaluate your goals, and make adjustments so you can reach these goals. While it's important to get started, it's just as important to ensure you are taking the most effective steps to reach your goals and identify what is and what is not working. Writing out your goals makes them real, but if you aren't sitting down to review your progress, it will be easy to completely forget and neglect them.

Every year you should sit down with your partner or by yourself to look over your finances. When you do, be sure to ask:

1. How well were you able to manage your spending and savings?
2. What were you able to achieve?
3. Are your current financial goals still relevant and realistic?
4. Do you need to make any revisions to your goals? Why? And how?

5. What is motivating you to stay committed to your current goals, both internally and externally?

6. Do you need to seek out professional advice? This can be to help establish new opportunities or to review more complex issues you might be having with your finances.

Be flexible and patient with your goals. But also remember that you need to have the right discipline and mindset to stay committed. As you review your financial progress, also check in with your mindset and be honest about some of the things you might be doing that are hindering your progress.

Chapter Highlights

- Maintain the right mindset to reach your personal and financial goals.
- Set SMART goals.
- Reviewing your goals is just as important as setting your goals.
- Schedule in time for yourself to review your progress, and do not forget to sit down with your partner to ensure you both are on the same page financially.

Afterword

Historically, financial independence is something that many women have not had thanks to society preventing a woman from having the opportunity to manage her own money. We are so much more fortunate today. Now there are many ways for women to gain financial independence. All women, whether married or single, can work towards being financially independent. This book has provided you with a number of ways to grow your money and take ownership of Your life.

While you do this, it's important to be kind to yourself. Don't beat yourself up about past mistakes you may have made. Whatever you think those mistakes are, they're in the past and there really is no point. You're moving forwards and upwards now.

Also remember that financial independence is not something that requires extensive financial skills. Tracking your spending can be an eye-opening experience that will help you identify poor spending habits and find ways to break those habits or create new, better ones. This is the first step to understanding your own financial literacy. From this tracking, you plan and create a budget. Creating a budget will allow you to take a serious look at your finances, determine what you should be spending in different areas, and ensure that you follow your planned expenditures. Next, you want to look at your future. What are your goals for retirement? What do you need to ensure your children are taken care of?

As you have learned, investing can be intimidating, but there are many different ways to invest. Take some time to research them and make some decisions that will work best for you while affording you the opportunity to prepare for your future. Finally, getting out of debt is a crucial step to financial independence. Make a plan. Start with one account at a time and work toward paying off your debts. When you do, you'll free up some income to put toward other investments and necessities that you and your family need.

Allow yourself the time to think about where you want to be with your finances. Make realistic goals that are measurable and will help you reach your ultimate goal of financial independence and freedom. Sit down with your partner and become a team. Work together to reach the goals you both want for yourself and for your family.

Those who are financially independent are more confident and take action to achieve their goals, whether financial or otherwise. Knowing you are capable of managing the household if something were to happen to your partner is an empowering feeling. You notice that your desire to achieve more in other areas of your life and be a role model to your children becomes a primary focus. You learn to live life on your terms without the extra stress or anxiety that comes from being dependent on your partner for most things.

Financial independence is an attainable goal for anyone. Just remember to take it one step at a time. This book has outlined all the steps to take. Now you just have to take them. I know you can do it!

And lastly ...

If you enjoyed this book I would love it if you could please leave a review on your local Amazon store. This will help other women like you find their way to the book and start taking control of their finances too.

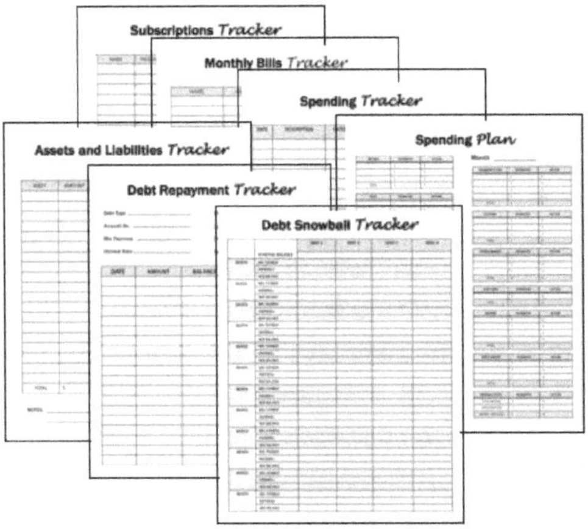

Get Your Free Budget Planner Bundle

Take the guesswork out of where your money is going and start planning how to make it work for you.

- The Budget Planner Bundle is a set of templates to help you work out your current financial position, track your spending, put together a budget/spending plan and pay down debts
- Designed to be used while reading this book
- Choose from color or black and white
- Can be printed on US letter size or A4 size paper.

Download your free Budget Planner Bundle and start smart budgeting today. Go to www.zoemadden.com

References

Caldwell, M. (2021a, July 7). *Has your partner put you on an allowance? When it's OK & when it's not.* The Balance. https://www.thebalance.com/what-if-my-spouse-gives-me-an-allowance-or-house-money-2385588

Caldwell, M. (2021b, July 10). *5 things you should do before you begin investing.* The Balance. https://www.thebalance.com/before-you-begin-investing-five-things-to-consider-2386111

Covert, B. (2012, March 21). *The high cost of being a woman.* The Nation. https://www.thenation.com/article/archive/high-cost-being-woman/

Cox, C., CFP®, & CRPC®. (2017, September 26). *Get "SMART" with your personal financial goals.* Wealthspire. https://www.wealthspire.com/blog/get-smart-personal-financial-goals/

Cruze, R. (2021, August 26). *15 practical budgeting tips.* Ramsey Solutions. https://www.ramseysolutions.com/budgeting/the-truth-about-budgeting

Daugherty, G. (2021, February 15). *The history of the gender wage gap in America.* Investopedia. https://www.investopedia.com/history-gender-wage-gap-america-5074898

Easr, S. (2021, July 23). *Financial help for women in abusive relationships.* MoneyGeek. https://www.moneygeek.com/financial-planning/resources/financial-help-women-abusive-relationships/

Egan, J. (2020, August 2). *5 bad money habits and how to break them.* Experian. https://www.experian.com/blogs/ask-experian/bad-money-habits-and-how-to-break-them/

Eneriz, A. (2021, April 28). *Debt avalanche vs. debt snowball: What's the difference?* Investopedia. https://www.investopedia.com/articles/personal-finance/080716/debt-avalanche-vs-debt-snowball-which-best-you.asp

Freeman, A. (2021, June 30). *9 money saving tips for families & households on a budget.* Money Crashers. https://www.moneycrashers.com/money-saving-tips-families/

Irby, L. (2021, May 9). *7 reasons it is so hard to get out of debt.* The Balance. https://www.thebalance.com/hard-to-pay-off-debt-960855

Janmohamed, S. (n.d.). *Financial independence remains a challenge for women all over the world.* The National. https://www.thenationalnews.com/opinion/comment/financial-independence-remains-a-challenge-for-women-all-over-the-world-1.890772

Jespersen, C. (2020, December 15). *5 steps for tracking your monthly expenses.* NerdWallet. https://www.nerdwallet.com/article/finance/tracking-monthly-expenses

Kagan, J. (2021, February 21). *Personal spending plan definition.* Investopedia. https://www.investopedia.com/terms/p/personal-spending-plan.asp

LaPonsie, M. (2021, July 19). *What is a testamentary trust and how do I create one?* US News & World Report; U.S. News & World Report. https://money.usnews.com/money/personal-finance/family-finance/articles/whats-a-testamentary-trust-and-how-do-i-create-one

Lewis-Parks, A. (2019, August 8). *Asking 10 experts: The challenges women face with money.* Consolidated Credit. https://www.consolidatedcredit.org/financial-news/challenges-women-face-with-money/

McGee, S., & Moore, H. (2014, August 11). *Women's rights and their money: a timeline from Cleopatra to Lilly Ledbetter.* The Guardian. https://www.theguardian.com/money/us-money-blog/2014/aug/11/women-rights-money-timeline-history

Mitchell, C. (2020, October 29). *Personal financial statement definition and example.* Investopedia. https://www.investopedia.com/terms/p/personal-financial-statement.asp

Mutual funds. (n.d.). Investor.gov. https://www.investor.gov/introduction-investing/investing-basics/investment-products/mutual-funds-and-exchange-traded-1

NerdWallet. (2020, December 21). *The 7 best budget apps for 2021.* https://www.nerdwallet.com/article/finance/best-budget-apps

O'Shea, A., & Lam-Balfour, T. (2021, August 17). *Beginner investing: 6 ways to get started.* NerdWallet. https://www.nerdwallet.com/article/investing/investments-for-beginners

O'Shea, B. (2021, August 5). *Debt relief: Understand your options and the consequences.* NerdWallet. https://www.nerdwallet.com/article/finance/find-debt-relief

Pant, P. (2021, August 15). *3 strategies for combining finances when engaged or moving in together.* The Balance. https://www.thebalance.com/three-methods-for-co-mingling-a-couple-s-finances-453849

Robyn, C. (2021, July 19). *6 reasons why you should start investing right now* Earnest Blog Money Advice for Young Professionals. https://www.earnest.com/blog/6-reasons-to-start-investing-now/

Rose, J. (2021, August 20). *The top 10 good financial goals that everyone should have for 2021.* Good Financial Cents®. https://www.goodfinancialcents.com/good-financial-goals/

Think Money. (2014, November 28). *8 reasons it can be hard to stick to a budget.* Thinkmoney. https://www.thinkmoney.co.uk/blog/8-reasons-it-can-be-hard-to-stick-to-a-budget/

What's the difference between saving and investing? (n.d.) . MaPS. https://www.moneyhelper.org.uk/en/savings/how-to-save/should-i-save-or-invest?source=mas#

Wikipedia Contributors. (2021, July 15). *Hetty Green.* Wikimedia Foundation. https://en.wikipedia.org/wiki/Hetty_Green

Wong, K. (2017, May 9). *The annoying psychology of why you can't stick to a budget.* The Cut. https://www.thecut.com/2017/05/the-annoying-psychology-of-why-you-cant-stick-to-a-budget.html

Yochim, D., & Coombes, A. (2021, August 23). *Best retirement plans: Choose the right account for you.* NerdWallet.

About the Author

Zoe Madden is a qualified nutritionist, kinesiologist, engineer, financial planner, writer and editor. This weird combination means she's not only the poster girl for career reinvention, but has a wealth of experience to draw on when it comes to health, wellbeing, and staying sane in this crazy world.

Zoe's passion is honoring mind, body and spirit to bring about balance. She favors clean, green and natural options wherever possible but doesn't advocate rigidly sticking to any particular practice or health regime. She believes what matters most is finding what works for you in this exciting ride that is Motherhood. Her books are intended to be resources to help you do just that. Visit Zoe at www.zoemadden.com.

Also By Zoe

Stop Putting Yourself Last: The Self-Care Book For Moms

Be the Best Mom AND Live the Life You Want

Discover the secret to practicing self-care, even if you don't have a minute to spare...

Are you used to feeling like you're running on empty?

As rewarding as being a mom is, it can also be an exhausting, thankless experience at times. To make matters worse, it seems like every other mom you know has her life pulled together, and you find yourself wondering why they can do it but you can't.

It's time to change all that. In *Stop Putting Yourself Last* you'll discover why taking care of you is so important. You really can move on from the guilt, the mom shaming, and the idea we're not doing enough or even good enough.

To be the best mom you can be, you have to learn how to prioritize your own needs without sacrificing the needs of your family.

Here is just a fraction of what you will discover:

- How to navigate the ups and downs of motherhood without guilt, shame, or self-blame

- Proven stress relief practices that will help you reclaim your time and mental peace, even with the busiest of schedules
- Tips and tricks for developing better habits, eating healthier, and moving your body
- How to feel calmer, stronger and more able to cope with everyday life
- How to accept yourself exactly as you are and recognize your own self-worth as a person and a mother.

And much more.

When you start showing up for yourself, you'll be amazed at the ripple effect it has on your life, relationships, and responsibilities. These simple self-love practices are designed to fit into your busy daily routine so you can begin making changes today and start living the life you want.

Stop Putting Yourself Last is available on Amazon. Scan the QR code to go to your local Amazon store.

Made in United States
Troutdale, OR
11/03/2026

56844709R00066